1919

THE YEAR THINGS FELL APART?

1919
THE YEAR THINGS FELL APART?

Edited and introduced by John Lack

for the History Fellows and Associates
School of Historical and Philosophical Studies
University of Melbourne

Australian Scholarly

Lack, John 1941–

First published 2019 by
Australian Scholarly Publishing Pty Ltd
7 Lt Lothian St Nth, North Melbourne, Vic 3051
Tel: 03 9329 6963 / Fax: 03 9329 5452
enquiry@scholarly.info / www.scholarly.info

ISBN 978-1-925984-15-6

Cover design: Wayne Saunders

Contents

Acknowledgements

In 2019 the History Fellows and Associates of the School of Historical and Philosophical Studies (SHAPS) at the University of Melbourne decided to focus their annual Research Day on the theme *1919: the year things fell apart?* On 19 July our new Head of School, Professor Margaret Cameron, opened the day with a stimulating address on the importance of history, and Dr Juliet Flesch soon had us talking, with 'I wish I had known that', a reflection on the serendipity of her lifetime of reading and research. Fellows and Associates read seven papers, and the Convenors invited them to submit them for publication. I am grateful to Tony Ward and Ross McMullin for offering additional papers, which I readily accepted, and for delivering them promptly at short notice.

The Fellows' and Associates' scholarship is supported by the vital collections held in such places as State Library Victoria and the library of the University of Melbourne, and we express our gratitude to their specialist librarians. I thank the Convenors and authors for entrusting me with managing this project, and Val Noone and Fay Woodhouse for their copyediting and warm support.

Nick Walker of Australian Scholarly Publishing responded enthusiastically to the idea of a collection on the theme of 1919, and – hey, presto! – here it is.

John Lack
9 October 2019

The Second Coming

Turning and turning in the widening gyre
The falcon cannot hear the falconer;
Things fall apart; the centre cannot hold;
Mere anarchy is loosed upon the world,
The blood-dimmed tide is loosed, and everywhere
The ceremony of innocence is drowned;
The best lack all conviction, while the worst
Are full of passionate intensity.

Surely some revelation is at hand;
Surely the Second Coming is at hand.
The Second Coming! Hardly are those words out
When a vast image out of Spiritus Mundi
Troubles my sight: somewhere in sands of the desert
A shape with lion body and the head of a man,
A gaze blank and pitiless as the sun,
Is moving its slow thighs, while all about it
Reel shadows of the indignant desert birds.
The darkness drops again; but now I know
That twenty centuries of stony sleep
Were vexed to nightmare by a rocking cradle,
And what rough beast, its hour come round at last,
Slouches towards Bethlehem to be born?

William Butler Yeats

Written in 1919 in the aftermath of the Great War and at the beginning of the Irish War of Independence, and first published in 1920.

Introduction

Was 1919 the year when, to adapt Yeats' words, 'things fell apart and the centre could not hold'? The people of Europe had not wanted war in 1914, but they got a war that became the Great War; they wanted peace in 1919, but the Versailles Conference and Treaty gave them, not a lasting peace, but only an uneasy truce that began to collapse in a little over a decade. The negatives of 1919 have been blamed for many of the ills of the subsequent century, but how responsible were those negatives for the calamities that followed?

'Almost all memoirs, diaries and letters from the period,' American historian Michael Neiberg asserts in *Dance of the Furies,* his challenging study of the onset of the Great War, 'expressed extreme shock, sadness, and fear at the outbreak of war.' The war was not initially a people's war, he insists, but rather a war instigated by a score or so of military and diplomatic leaders out of touch with the people, few of whom were expecting war and even fewer wanting war. In 1914, class, gender, ethnicity and religion were more important to people's identity than nationality. Political and social movements, and the convictions and prejudices they embodied, were already transnational in character, but calls to patriotism fractured them.

Europeans went to war in August 1914, determinedly if not enthusiastically, because they were led to believe that making war was defensive rather than offensive, that any war would be limited, and that its burdens would be borne equitably. In March-April 1915 Sigmund Freud divined Europe's mood unerringly:

> the war in which we had refused to believe broke out, and it brought – disillusionment. Not only is it more bloody

> and more destructive [and] at least as cruel, as embittered, as implacable as any that preceded it ... It tramples in blind fury on all that comes its way, as though there were to be no future and no peace among men after it is over. It cuts all the common bonds between the contending peoples, and threatens to leave a legacy of embitterment that will make any renewal of those bonds impossible for a long time to come.

Europe continued to fight for some four years because the shocking casualties of November–December 1914 created venomous hatreds that made only total victory acceptable. While 1917 was the costliest for Australia, 1914 was by far the deadliest of the war overall: Germany lost 116,000 killed and 400,000 wounded on the Western Front, amounting to almost one-third of all German casualties in that theatre for the entire war; France sacrificed 329,000 dead in the first two months alone. The 1918 Armistice brought a sense of relief, but that relief did not everywhere last very long. Looked at another way, the Great War was a nationalist-imperialistic interregnum that gave pre-war class, ethnic and religious loyalties a national focus, translating them into lethal cocktails of animosity that were, in the post-war era of nation-state 'self-determination', to breed unrest, protest, revolt, revolution and counter revolution.

By the end of 1919 many prominent thinkers and publicists, from dangerous cranks to rational and informed observers, had expressed their dismay at the course world events had taken since 1914. Six months into the war Freud had been aghast: 'We had expected the great world-dominating nations of white race upon whom the leadership of the human species has fallen, who were known to have world-wide interests as their concern, to whose creative powers were due not only our technical advances towards the control of nature but the artistic and scientific standards of civilization – we had expected these people to succeed in discovering another way of settling misunderstandings and conflicts of interest.' Far less high-minded than Freud was Lothrop Stoddard, a Harvard-educated pseudo-'scientific racist' and white supremacist who wrote, in *The Rising Tide of Color Against White*

World-Supremacy (1920), of the Great War as a calamity for the superior white ('Nordic') race that he regarded as under siege from the 'yellows, browns, blacks and reds'. The war, a 'death-grapple' between European nations, had been 'nothing short of a headlong plunge into white race-suicide ... essentially a civil war between closely related white stocks; a war wherein every physical and mental effective was gathered up and hurled into a hell of lethal machinery which killed out unerringly the youngest, the bravest, and the best'. The material damage to European civilization was so huge as to be incalculable, Stoddard lamented, and the vital losses stupefying: 60 million mobilised for war, 33 million casualties (including 8 million killed or dead from disease, 19 million wounded, and seven million prisoners). The science of industrial war – chemical and mechanical – had miniaturised and pulverised its puny players.

Freud perceived that the war, as well as causing disillusionment, was changing attitudes to death: 'we are not able to maintain our former attitude towards death, and have not yet found a new one'. Deaths were no longer occurring singly, accidentally, and from the normal effluxion of time, but in masses, intentionally, and among the young. How were the world's bereaved to mourn death on this scale, and with the dead killed far from home, most of them never identified or even found? In this collection I have interpreted the 1919 diary of an Australian father coming to terms with the death of a son whose grave he could never visit. But at least Frank Roberts had a grave. More than half of the British Empire's million war dead were buried in nameless graves – 'A Soldier of the Great War / Known Unto God' – or merely listed on massive memorials to the 'Missing'. On 11 November 1918 a profound silence descended on the world's bereaved, a moment marked thereafter in the British Empire on that date by a two-minute silence before the empty sepulchre of the London Cenotaph, joined in 1920 by an 'unknown warrior', interred in Westminster Abbey. The dying did not stop with the Armistice, for the war was followed by a pandemic of 'Spanish' pneumonic influenza, responsible for at least 50 million deaths. As **Anthea Hyslop** explains, distance was no tyrant to Australia but a godsend that, together with medical precautions, helped to reduce the ravages of influenza. Nevertheless, 14,000 Australians died, equivalent to almost 25 per cent of the nation's war deaths. While there was cooperation at community level and much volunteering, there was anything but consensus and cooperation between federal and state governments once the flu eluded quarantine.

The Great War was regarded as having the most appalling dysgenic effect in robbing the world, especially the European world, of its fittest, brightest and noblest generation. According to this view, war had cost the human gene pool its healthiest, most intelligent and patriotic men, and preserved on the home front the timid, the weak and the disabled. If, as some said, Anzac had 'made Australia a nation', what sort of nation was it in 1919? For herein lay the post-war belief in a 'lost generation' succeeded by degenerates, and social tensions between 'loyalists' who had served their country and the disparaged 'slackers' who had squibbed their duty. Such thinking bolstered ultra patriots who favoured employment preference, housing support, business loans, and land settlement for returned soldiers, whose votes they courted, and it also gave a fillip to eugenists who advocated selective birth control and sterilisation of the 'unfit'. Lothrop Stoddard regarded Australia's White Australia policy as an exemplary example of white Pacific nations and regions determined by means of prohibitive legislation to preserve their 'racial purity'. But there was a fear in Australia that the costs of war, combined with a declining birth rate, threatened long-term prospects for national rebuilding to resist alien invasion. Here **Fay Woodhouse** tells of the Australian equation of birth control with 'race suicide', and the instructive story of the banning of Marie Stopes' eugenic birth control book *Wise Parenthood.*

1919 was the year of repatriation, of the homecoming of the survivors. Tens of thousands of them, especially those from the British Dominions and notably in Australia and New Zealand, had been in Europe for years – for the duration of the war, in fact. Disoriented, damaged physically and mentally, and diseased, as many of them were, their reintegration into family, employment and community life proved challenging. Economies were disrupted, trade and production awry, and unemployment high. In

Australia, as perhaps elsewhere, veterans faced the suspicion of unionists who feared the politicians' promise of job preference for returning men. Where would veterans' loyalties lie? With their class, or with the nation? Some veterans clashed with unionists and radical activists and socialists. Across the British Empire, Peace Day 19 July 1919 was marred by veteran protests, even violence. **Ross McMullin** tells how in Melbourne returned soldiers' unrest and police over-reaction led to a spectacular example of violence involving the Victorian Premier. During 1916–1917 Australia had been bitterly divided over proposals for military conscription, industrial coercion, the high cost of living, and the socially inequitable burden of war. The Great Strike of 1917 had caused massive disruption and suffering, but the year after the war saw the worst-ever level of industrial disputation. This is the context of **Carolyn Rasmussen**'s examination of the role of lawyer and Labor leader Maurice Blackburn in settling the massive seamen's strike of 1919 and achieving significant pay increases and working condition reforms.

Confrontation, negotiation, compromise and concession generally marked the negotiations of the Allied victors' representatives who assembled at the Versailles Conference in the first six months of 1919, attempting to define mutually satisfactory peace terms to dictate to Germany. To put it mildly, Versailles – Conference and Treaty – have not enjoyed a good press. Stoddard saw Europe's Great War as the world's Second Peloponnesian War, the first having destroyed Greek civilisation, for the peace that followed had been no harbinger of amity but 'a mere truce, dictated by the victor of the moment to sullen and vengeful enemies ... infused with no healing or constructive virtue, [and] but the first of a war cycle which completed Hellas's ruin'. Crude as Stoddard's views of 1914–1918 as a form of race suicide were, they probably struck a popular chord: 'Armageddon engendered Versailles; earth's worst war closed with an unconstructive peace which left old sores unhealed and even dealt fresh wounds.' The Versailles Conference proved something of an arm-wrestle between U.S. President Wilson's obdurate idealism – 'Peace without victory' – and French President Clemenceau's equally obstinate demand for revenge, reparations and security. John Maynard Keynes, who was the financial representative

THE TIGER: "Curious! I seem to hear a child weeping!"

'Peace and Future Cannon Fodder'. Will Dyson's most famous cartoon, published in the London *Herald* on 17 May 1919, shows the Big Four (Lloyd George, Vittorio Orlando, 'The Tiger' Georges Clemenceau, and Woodrow Wilson) after signing the Peace Treaty.

of the British Treasury at Versailles, resigned in disgust at the Treaty, not at the criminal articles or the war-guilt clause, but with the reparation demands, which he regarded as breaching international law and threatening the long-term economic health of Central Europe. The victors had fought the war 'ostensibly waged in defense of international engagements', only to eschew them in conference: 'There are few episodes in history which posterity will have less reason to condone'. As **Tony Ward** points out, in examining Australian PM Hughes' role in stiffening increased demands for German war reparations, Keynes' book *The Economic Consequences of the Peace* (published late in 1919), with its criticism of the 'Carthaginian Peace', dealt the reputation of Versailles a shattering blow, the long-term effects of which are still being debated.

Behind Keynes' concerns for a just treaty lay a wish for a durable European peace; behind Stoddard's lament for a poor outcome at Versailles lay a fear of future European wars that would vitiate the white world-supremacy that his racist paranoia told him was already under attack from over-breeding and geographically mobile inferior peoples. He regretted that the belligerents had enlisted their 'colored' colonies to bolster their armies and labour corps, for this had given inferior races a ringside seat at the war that constituted Europe's near-death rattle. The only development that Stoddard believed warranted further war, and that immediately, was war against the 'monstrous insanities of Bolshevism' that threatened 'the death or degradation of nearly all persons displaying constructive ability, and the tyranny of the ignorant and anti-social element'. Bolshevism, in this view, 'would be the most gigantic triumph of disgenics ever seen'.

Stoddard could not see that the protracted nature of the Versailles Conference, while Europe slid into chaos, and the hypocrisy of the victors, who denied any measure of justice to colonised peoples who had made sacrifices to defeat Prussian militarism, lay at the heart of increasing restiveness, within and outside Europe. Vladimir Lenin advocated nations' rights to self-determination; by contrast, President Wilson accepted colonial possessions, advocating liberal national rights only for countries that were outside colonial empires and that were not colonial possessions.

It is also salutary to remember that Woodrow Wilson was a Southern white racist, and that the United States was an imperial power. The Treaty gave 'self-determination' only to some of the peoples of the dismembered vanquished Empires, and was therefore a huge disappointment to those denied consideration – the Irish and the Koreans, for instance – and to the people of the victors' colonies in Africa, Asia and the Pacific, who were refused any concessions, despite their contributions to the Allied war effort. Instead the victors proceeded to divide the spoils of war in the Middle East and the former German colonies. In his challenging large-canvas essay, **David Palmer** examines upheavals and reactions in the three regions of East Asia, America, and Europe, exploring the global linkages between empires, revolutions, and the origins of fascism, and the role played by big business in the dynamic shifts that occurred in 'the era of 1919'.

While the Great War remained a desperate struggle for national survival, domestic enemies could remain united in facing the enemy. But when hostilities ceased, unrest erupted in protest, mutiny, rebellion and revolution against the immense sufferings and unequal sacrifices that war brought. Class, ethnic and religious differences were re-energised by war and suffering. The Great War, Neiberg comments, 'is a reminder to us all that wars have tendencies to take on lives of their own and to destroy even those who ostensibly win them'. Yet from Belgium, the innocent bystander nation that became the terrible first casualty of the Great War, there emerged, as **Val Noone** explains, a movement of Christian and social democratic orientation, the Young Catholic Workers. Under the leadership of Joseph Cardijn, the YCW was part of a worldwide upsurge in labour activism. Not all things were falling apart or beyond renewal. Were there signs of healing, too, in the behaviour of the world community of scientists? In 1915 a disillusioned Sigmund Freud had written 'Science herself has lost her passionless impartiality; her deeply embittered servants seek for weapons from her with which to contribute towards the struggle with the enemy.' **Rod Home**'s paper on the 1919 testing of Albert Einstein's theory of relativity, introduces us, cautiously but engagingly, to the subject of the thawing of the wartime fervour that, infecting many scientists, had undercut time-honoured ideals about the internationalism of science.

There persists a common person-in-the-street attitude that the Great War led inexorably to the second World War. Two closing points:

There were chilling trans-Atlantic continuities and transferences in the interwar period. German national socialists certainly drew support from American race supremacists such as Lothrop Stoddard and his forerunner and backer Madison Grant. Stoddard's book was reprinted several times after his exposure as a member of the KKK in 1922, the same year that his new book *The Revolt Against Civilization: The Menace of the Under-man* introduced the term *untermensch* into Nazi racial theory. Grant contributed to U.S. immigration restriction and anti-miscegenation laws and when the Nazis came to power, *The Passing of the Great Race* was the first non-German book ordered to be printed. In F. Scott Fitzgerald's *The Great Gatsby* (1925), his numbskull character Tom Buchanan extolled the writings of 'this man Goddard' (an amalgam of Grant and Stoddard). Fitzgerald poked fun, but neither Grant nor Stoddard was a humourist. Nor for that matter was Buchanan, a man given to casually cruel treatment of his social inferiors. No siree.

Were the Great War and the war's aftermath responsible for the march to war in the 1930s? American intervention and post-war economic dominance, Adam Tooze argues in *The Deluge* (2014), encouraged the startling explosion of violence in the 1930s and 1940s: 'It was precisely the looming potential, the future dominance of American capitalistic democracy, that was the common factor impelling Hitler, Stalin, the Italian fascists and their Japanese counterparts to such radical action'. One rejoinder might be that the American refusal to endorse the Wilsonian peace, however much it had been compromised, ushered in a long period of disengagement from Europe, amounting no less to isolationism. My argument, then, comes full circle, for that American refusal and the consequential fatal power void were anchored in 1919, the year in which 'things fell apart'.

John Lack

A note on sources

A. Scott Berg, *Wilson* (New York: Berkley Books, 2014).

Michael S. Neiberg, *Dance of the Furies: Europe and the Outbreak of World War* (Cambridge, Massachusetts: Harvard University Press, 2011), 5, 237.

Adam Tooze, *The Deluge: The Great War, America and the Remaking of the Global Order, 1916–1931* (London and New York: Viking Penguin, 2014), 7.

Sigmund Freud: 'Thoughts for the Times on War and Death: I The Disillusionment of the War, II Our Attitude Towards Death ' in *The Standard Edition of the Complete Psychological Works of Sigmund Freud,* Vol. XIV (London: The Hogarth Press and the Institute of Psycho-Analysis, 1957).

John Maynard Keynes is quoted from Larry Zuckerman, *The Rape of Belgium: The Untold Story of World War I* (New York and London: New York University Press, 2004), 259.

Lothrop Stoddard: *The Rising Tide of Color Against White World-Supremacy* (New York: The Scribner Press; London: Chapman and Hall, 1920) came with an introduction-endorsement by his fellow 'scientific racist' Madison Grant, author of *The Passing of the Great Race; or, The Racial Basis of European History* (1917). The term 'disgenic' (or dysgenic), had been coined as the opposite of 'eugenic' by the American eugenist and pacifist, David Starr Jordon, author of *The Blood of the Nation* (1902, expanded edition 1910) and *What War Really Means* (1913). See also Jonathan P. Spiro, *Defending the Master Race: Conservation, Eugenics, and the Legacy of Madison Grant* (University Press of New England, 2008).

Accurate Great War casualties are elusive, but Stoddard's figures are fairly close to the careful and conservative modern conclusions of Joseph E. Persico, *Eleventh Month, Eleventh Day, Eleventh Hour: Armistice Day, 1918: World War I and Its Violent Climax* (New York: Random House, 2004), 379–80 and his Appendix: 8,364,000 deaths; 21,436,000 wounded (of whom seven million were permanently maimed); and 6,276,000 civilian deaths. By contrast Stoddard asserted civilian deaths from hunger, exposure, disease, massacre and heightened infant mortality were five times those of military deaths.

Heartbreak House

'Eumana', Hastings Road, Upper Hawthorn

JOHN LACK

On this date, one hundred years ago – 19 July 1919 – at about this moment,* Australians were preparing to observe Peace Day, a public holiday throughout the British Empire celebrating the signing of the Treaty of Versailles.

That evening John Roberts, chief accountant to the Melbourne Tramway & Omnibus Company, living at 'Eumana' (resting place), 17 Hastings Road, Upper Hawthorn, wrote in his diary: 'Peace Day – Frank arrived in England 2 years ago. I went to [the] office till 10 then to [the] Bank (Comml) with [the] Boards money and afterwards home saw a little of the march past near [Spencer Street] Railway St[atio]n 5 aeroplanes overhead. In [the] afternoon [I] cut papers and in [the] evening pasted them and photos in [the] record Book'. Four days later he visited Army Base Records in Melbourne to collect a box containing Frank's effects ('memorials of my dear and gallant son'), and on Wednesday 23rd, he noted 'This would have been Frank's birthday age 31'. On 26 July he pasted into his diary a newspaper article on 'Peace Day' expressing bitterness towards those who had sacrificed nothing to the war effort and written by a parent whose 'share in peace ... means ... two narrow mounds of earth somewhere in France'.

* This paper was read to the Fellows' Research Day on the morning of 19 July 2019.

'No form of expression more emphatically embodies the expresser'

John Roberts had been keeping a diary since 1879, but only those for 1915–1922 are in public hands.[1] The diaries he wrote after his son's death in September 1918 have become perhaps the sources most quoted by historians of bereavement in Australia.[2] Thomas Mallon suggests that diaries are written not so much for the self, as for an audience, and are therefore shaped by that anticipated readership.[3] Roberts' diary has an air about it resembling what Katie Homes has described as 'a means of ordering experience and establishing control over one's life'.[4] It certainly conveys John Roberts' anxiety about keeping tabs on the members of his family: his wife Roberta (Berta) Roberts, their 27-year-old daughter Gwen (engaged in home duties), their 16-year-old schoolboy son Bert, and their daughter-in-law Ruby and her baby Nancy, the widow and daughter of Frank who exactly four months earlier had been killed in action in France. Mallon again: 'One can read a poem or a novel without coming to know its author, look at a painting and fail to get a sense of its painter ... one cannot read a diary and feel unacquainted with its writer. No form of expression more emphatically embodies the expresser: diaries are the flesh made word.'[5] Is this true? We will find that historians have reached quite different understandings of the diarist John Roberts. Diaries may beguile historians, but they are hardly unproblematic as sources.

On 11 November 1918 the grieving Roberts had received the news of the armistice with mixed feelings. John wrote 'A year and a half since dear old Frank sailed for the War, and that war took him.' When he returned to work the next day 'A lot of the girls at the office gathered around me and sang "for he's a jolly good fellow".' His diary entry ended: 'With all the jollification around the sting is that dear old Frank won't come back.' Roberts and his brother Will, chairman of the Melbourne Stock Exchange, considered the truce premature; wanting Germany crushed and humiliated, they opposed a negotiated peace. Their sons' deaths, in 1915 at Gallipoli and in 1918 in France, had deepened their hatred of Germany. On 24 July

1919 John pasted into his diary a news cutting reporting the cheering that punctuated Will's words at the Stock Exchange: 'to Great Britain and her allies ... was the pride of victory ... Right had triumphed over might. The peace terms were drastic but it was a peace of justice and not of revenge'.[6]

John Roberts' parents were Irish Protestant emigrants who prospered at storekeeping, and mine management and speculation at Scarsdale before moving their family to Ballarat, where their two sons John and Will began careers in, respectively, accountancy and share management. The brothers were particularly close, for they had been only schoolchildren when their mother, suffering postnatal depression, drowned herself at St Kilda. Their father's second marriage was a happy one (John enjoyed startling friends with his boast that he had been best man at his father's wedding) and the union gave the boys several half siblings. John and Will settled near one another in the comfortable middle-class suburbs of Upper Hawthorn and Kew. In 1919 John was slated to become manager of the entire cable network of the emerging Tramways Board, on an annual salary of £750; Will was in his 15th year as chairman of the Melbourne Stock Exchange.[7]

John's diary generally records the minutiae of his days. He fills the allotted space (three days to a page), pastes in overlapping press clippings, and glues in extra pages whenever he needs more space. Every day John chronicles, obsessively, the whereabouts of every member of his family, and lists the letters he sends and receives, the people he meets on the tram, who call on him at his city office, with whom he has lunch, and who visit him at home. Although he has been living at 'Eumana' since 1889, there are few references to neighbours. A busy, salaried company man, he has many artistic and literary friends, and is a bibliophile who fancies himself to be a member of Melbourne's 'bohemia'. He reads at least three daily newspapers, always has a novel or history nearby in the evening, and (before his son's death) goes to the theatre or a film several times each week.

Reading John Roberts' diary one would hardly be aware of the influenza pandemic raging in Melbourne in 1919. He mentions influenza only to record his own inoculations (two doses of serum having been sensibly provided to tramways staff at Head Office), and those of his family, and two visitors who were 'carriers', the condition of two or three hospitalised friends, and the isolation of his young son and granddaughter at 'Sunnyside', his weekender at South Sassafras (Kallista, today) in the Dandenongs. Otherwise the epidemic might almost not be happening. He commutes as usual to his City office, and lunches at his habitual dining rooms and restaurants. Furthermore, apart from mentioning the cancellation of evening trams to save power, Roberts' diary gives barely a hint of the industrial strife then plaguing Melbourne. Tens of thousands of Melbourne people went short of food and warmth that winter.

Nor did Roberts give much attention to world news in 1919. During most of 1915–18 he was an armchair warrior, experiencing the war through the press, and the many war letters he received from family members, friends and serving tramway employees. He had noted in his diary some of the major battles in Europe, and glued press accounts into his scrapbooks (about which, more below), but these were rarely annotated, and he appears to have accepted without question the optimistic coverage of the progress of the war, despite his awareness of many casualties whose death notices he collected. On 16 March 1917 he had noted 'Word of Revolution in Russia and abdication of the Czar what does it mean?' and the next day 'News of Russian Revolution very promising', echoing *The Age* report, inserted in his diary, of the 'struggle for freedom from despotism'. There were no further references.

His 1919 diary was dominated by the news he received in September 1918 on what he described as 'the most awful day in our lives' – the news that his son Frank had been killed in action. This became the pivotal event of John's subsequent diaries, which since 1999 have attracted the attention of many historians: notably Joy Damousi (1999) and Pat Jalland (2002 and 2006), but also those writing more extensively about the Roberts – Tanja Luckins (2004) and Peter Stanley (2009).[8] Damousi and Jalland, pioneers of the study of war-related bereavement in Australia, handled the Roberts' diaries admirably, an approach summed up by Jalland's observation that, for Roberts, 'constructive grieving meant active memorialising through practical projects and peer group support which helped him work deliberately through sorrow'.[9] But there seemed to be more to Roberts' coming to terms with his loss than was suggested here. Some subsequent readings and interpretations of the diaries, following Damousi and Jalland's leads, have not satisfied my curiosity about Roberts' sustained depression. The historians work forward using the diaries, but they barely look back. Both Luckins' and Stanley's books, ambitious and stimulating as they are, misread, in my view, John Roberts' account of the day the news broke of his son's death, and they attempt to comprehend the father's long-term grief with scant reference to the nature of the father-son relationship that is revealed in the diaries preceding Frank's death. Their reading of the diaries (today joined by the 1922 diary) is also, at times, inattentive to significant detail.[10] 'The Roberts,' Tanja Luckins writes, 'will form something of a narrative thread in this book'.[11] But this thread, once tested against the diaries, quickly snaps. John Roberts learned of his son's death in somewhat harrowing circumstances, and both historians miss something vital to understanding the depth of the father's grief. With diaries, the devil is so often in the detail. Let us begin with Friday 13 September 1918, 'the most awful day' in the Roberts' lives.

'the last six days the worst of my life and yet the proudest'

That morning Berta and her son Bert left for 'Sunnyside', and John arrived at his City office about 10 am. John had been expecting, not what Luckins and Stanley describe as a telegram (an official telegram to Frank's widow was received by Gwen Roberts at Hawthorn from a clergyman at about 11 am), but a *cable*gram from Frank assuring him that, if all was not exactly quiet on the Western Front, he was still alive, perhaps uninjured: 'I noticed a cablegram as I thought on my desk ... It was a memo from the Eastern Extension Coy saying "I regret to inform you that London advises that your cablegram of the 14th August addressed to 6874 Roberts as being undelivered, the addressee having been killed in action."'[12] Such was the father's level of anxiety about Frank that, as well as showering him with money transfers (more than adequate to make Frank's periods of leave comfortable), and parcels of food, books and newspapers (that made him very popular in his Company and platoon), he had instituted a system of reply-paid cablegrams so that he could be regularly assured at his office of his son's safety. Instead, this arrangement had ensured that the news of Frank's death was received in the most matter-of-fact fashion.

'We know what [Frank's father] did and thought from his own account of that day,' Peter Stanley writes, 'preserved in a distracted scrawl in his bulky "Australia" 1918 diary.' Well, no, we don't necessarily know what John Roberts thought, because John's account was written six days later (as Luckins *does* note), and in a *clear and firm* hand on pages glued into the diary. Those pages convey what John had composed himself to write by 18 September. His account tells us more about what he *did* on 13 September (most importantly, how he confirmed the terrible news with Army Base Records) and what he subsequently *said*, rather than *how he felt* on hearing the news, other than that in the afternoon he 'felt very much upset positively sick with grief'.

Roberts went home to Hawthorn. 'What', Peter Stanley asks, 'did he do in that empty house between, say, 12.30 and about 6.30?' Well, as his diary records, the house was not empty – and he was not idle. Gwen was there with a family friend, Gwen's boyfriend visited, and Roberts wrote letters informing close friends of Frank's death. 'Later that afternoon,' Stanley continues, 'he regained his customary self-discipline and set out for Camberwell station.' But he was delayed in going to his wife at 'Sunnyside', not by grief, but by the fact that there was no train that would take him beyond Upper Fern Tree Gully a further three miles to Belgrave, for the shorter two-mile walk to 'Sunnyside', until the 6.35 from Flinders Street (6.58 from nearby Camberwell, arriving at Belgrave at 8.41).[13] He spent those hours at home, on the almost two-hour train trip to Belgrave, and on his walk to 'Sunnyside', steadying himself to speak that evening to his grieving wife (she most likely had taken Frank's most recent letter to Olinda that day), and next day to his shattered daughter-in-law.

When on 18 September Frank 'wrote up the awful diary of the last six days the worst of my life and yet the proudest', he described his son's death in words that ennobled its purpose as the death of 'our dear gallant soldier son' and 'my dear brave soldier son': 'I had to tell my brave son's brave mother that our first born had died a hero's death in France to help to save mankind. We were both distressed but proud of our son.' Subsequently he went to Olinda to comfort his daughter-in-law: '(Oh! We owe the Germans a lot)'. Assuring Ruby that 'as long as I had a roof over my head and a crust', she and her baby would share them, he sought to comfort her with the thought that 'the horrors of war might have sent [Frank] back home in a condition worse than death. With brain gone or so mangled that he might be a wreck only of his fine old self'. Better to be honouring a dead hero than greeting a maimed veteran?

Roberts went back to Hawthorn and busied himself with practical matters concerning Frank, including lodging death notices. His friend Guy Innes, editor of the *Herald,* published a short obituary 'The Goal Beyond The Prize' [Philippians 4:13] 'Lacrosseur Gives His Life ... after two years four months service ... [a man] endowed with a kindly humor and a quiet heroism [who] walked undismayed the ways of death'.[14]

What meaning was John Roberts to find in his son's death? One can readily infer from his diaries that Roberts had no religious faith, and this is confirmed by his diary entry for 19 June 1922: 'asked ... if I had the same belief I used to have (agnostic) ... I said yes'.[15]

It is starkly apparent that Frank's death left a great void in his father's life. On the first day of every month, John noted Frank's death. He also noted the anniversaries of Frank's enlistment, his leaving home, entry into camp, embarkation, arrival in England and in France, and his leave spent in Ireland, London, and Paris. The references are sometimes bleak: '2 years ago Frank left Eumana forever', sometimes written as 'for Ever'. His 1919 diary opened with 'NOTES FROM 1918: The Year of battle sudden death trouble and sickness, separation and worry' and 'Dear old Frank's body now in France'. And he kept every fragment related to his son, even pasting into his diary on 8 January 1919 a tattered piece of blank notepaper annotated 'This piece of paper came from dear old Frank'. Only the content of his diary changes, and not (as Luckins suggests) the format.[16] The reader opening the 1919 diary is immediately struck by his recurring activity: (New Year's Day) 'I was making cuttings from newspapers in evening ... I pasted in Cuttings in Record Books till after 12 pm did about 10 hours work'; (Friday 3 January) 'Gwen out in evening. I cut newspapers.' (More usually, 'Gwen out – again'.) And on Saturday 4 January: 'I went home [from work] in afternoon and cut newspapers in afternoon and evening'; (Sunday) 'I pasted cuttings in Record Books in afternoon and evening till after 12 am.' This went on day after day, month after month. Not until 1922 did he begin to resume his social life, and even then, slowly.

Having decided that Frank was a hero, Roberts began to amass evidence about his courageous war service and noble death. Berta Roberts, who remains a shadowy figure in her husband's diary (and hardly Luckins' 'something of a narrative replacement for his dead son'),[17] had immediately suggested 'getting a memorial of Frank printed'. John did this, but by late January 1919 he wrote of a 'proposed Memorial Book of Frank', began to correspond with Frank's army mates and their bereaved parents, and on 9 April wrote: 'During the day [at the office] I plotted out [the] plan for Frank's Memorial book.' He began amassing the records of Frank's birth, education, sporting achievements, and employment (as a bank clerk, and later as an orchardist at South Sassafras).

For John Roberts the compilation of scrapbooks was already a confirmed habit. A collector of theatrical ephemera from the 1880s, he began about 1894 to compile a personal encyclopaedia of press cuttings kept in huge 500-page Scrapbooks, on the arts in general, and the Federation movement. He had created 71 scrapbooks by 1905 and 150 by 1920, and built a library that eventually contained some 4000 books. 'These [scrap] books,' one amazed journalist observed of the whole collection in 1920, 'are the soul of a man.'[18] State Library Victoria holds 127 volumes, and manuscripts librarian Kevin Molloy suggests that 'the Roberts scrapbooks ... have become national icons'.[19] The Great War had compounded Roberts' obsessive collective instinct. He collected newspaper and magazine accounts of the major campaigns, and every year sent many hundreds of papers, journals and books to tramways employees and friends who had enlisted, pasting their return letters, postcards and photographs, along with cuttings from the Australian press, into a huge volume on Gallipoli, and then into volumes about the Western Front. He kept Frank supplied with funds for his visits on leave in Ireland, London and Paris. Frank reciprocated with scores of brochures, programmes, press cuttings and magazines, which his father avidly pasted into bulging scrapbooks. After Frank's death, John rearranged these mementoes to memorialise his son's months in the old world and in battle.[20]

'Dear old Frank': who saw him die?

John Roberts' immediate task was to find out exactly when and how Frank had died. Roberts knew from his nephew Private Lennard Roberts' death at Gallipoli that accounts penned by officers were not to be trusted: Lennard had been going about his normal duties when struck in the head by 'a stray bullet', an occurrence deeply lamented to a man by his comrades, especially as Lennard, despite his youth at 21, would soon have been promoted. Next morning his grave in Shrapnel Valley was found covered in snow.[21] The men of Frank's battalion, company and platoon wrote or called to tell how Frank had died storming a machine gun post at Mont St Quentin, but the accounts did not agree: one letter (provided by the Australian Red Cross Inquiry Department) said Frank had been killed by concussion, but the writer had not witnessed this, only buried him; another of the few survivors of 9 platoon, came to his city office and said (4 February), 'He was wounded by a bomb in the stomach Frank and he had gained the top of the Mount.' Private Dobson wrote (7 May) that 'Frank was hit by a bomb in the abdomen mortally wounding him. He died two minutes later', and called to tell that, at Frank's request, he straightened his legs and turned him on his back, 'and in a few minutes a yellow look came over Frank's face and he died'. Sgt Edwards of Frank's battalion had lunch with his father on 27 May: 'Edwards saw Frank when he was dead said he was shot through the chest [and] had blood over him'. After one such conversation his father wrote 'so passed, my dear, gallant son. I took Norrie and Dobson [his informants] to lunch at Carlyon's [Hotel]'.[22]

Roberts' language about Frank had changed: 'dear old Frank' of 1916–17 had become in 1918 'my dear, gallant son' and later 'my dear noble gallant son', transforming him into a saintly figure, and a hero of Mont St Quentin, a battle that the father would portray as a key to the Australian Corps' advance under Major General John Monash against the Hindenburg Line. On 1 September 1919 Roberts wrote: 'A year ago today my fine dear gallant son was killed in the capture of Mont St Quentin between 1 and 2 o'clock in the afternoon (Australian time between 11 and 12 pm.) A great feat of arms.' British General Rawlinson's measured praise – 'one of the finest feats of the war' – had become to Roberts and journalists (and later to some military historians) '*the* finest feat of the war'.

Searching for the evidence to sustain this image of Frank's war service and death meant interrogating returning veterans. Frank had written to his wife that 'some very fine reports of your fighting husband have been forwarded and received at Australian Corps Headquarters, and something is expected to come of it'. And some of Frank's mates *were* decorated for Mont St Quentin. Their testimony about the battle (as John Roberts saw their words) must be regarded with some caution, as they visited not only to convey their sympathy, but were often seeking work in a difficult post-war labour market. Roberts wrote them references, or recommended them to business contacts that might give them a try at the tramways, repair shops and factories. He took Frank's 'old mates' to lunch or dinner, singly and in groups, showing a particular interest in the survivors of Frank's platoon. He elicited written accounts of the battle for Mont St Quentin, badgering his informants for more and more detail, to the point of exhaustion. He wrote to grieving parents, enclosing copies of these sometimes-graphic accounts, and of official war photographs, including shots of the early common grave in which Frank and some of his comrades had been buried. His correspondents replied politely, but some were quite upset by the graphic details, and resisted, usually passively, Roberts' request for further details from their deceased sons' letters and diaries.[23] Roberts was not indifferent to the sadness of other bereaved parents – his diaries and scrapbooks are replete with death and in memoriam notices, and references to his sympathetic correspondence with the bereaved – it was just that in his pursuit of information about his own son, he could be most insensitive. Although he concedes Roberts' insensitivity, Peter Stanley builds *Men of Mont St Quentin,* his enterprising blend of family and military history, largely out of accounts that Roberts circulated among the men until, amended and re-amended, one suspects, he achieved, however consciously or unconsciously, the account of the platoon in action at Mont St Quentin that suited his purpose.

The image of Frank that he created, and the dedication with which he pursued that creation, testified to the intense nature of the father-son relationship forged before the son went to war. But that image of Frank as soldier-hero does not comfortably match the son presented in his father's diaries before Frank's death. Historians have hitherto largely ignored these diaries, and given little prominence to Frank's letters from the front.

The war comes home: anxiety and death in the Roberts' family

John Roberts' attitude to the war changed. Before Frank enlisted, his father was hoping for an early end to the war, and after Frank enlisted he became an even more fervent conscriptionist and a supporter of a protracted and crushing British victory. Indeed the families of John and Will Roberts appear to have been consumed by a war fervour that brought the war tragically home even before the deaths of their first-born sons. Will's son Lennard was serving at Gallipoli when he received terrible news from home in June 1915. One Sunday evening, two of his young brothers were playing heroes and spies. 'You be the German spy', one brother said, 'and I'll shoot you dead.' Picking up a pea rifle that he did not know was loaded, one boy shot his 9-year-old brother who died – a day later. Then there was the curious incident with John's 15-year-old son Bert in January 1918. Rabbiting at 'Sunnyside', and, demonstrating to a friend how *not* to climb through a fence carrying a rifle with one's hand over the muzzle, he did just that, and so blasted his thumb and near two fingers that they required amputation. Bert's first words to his father were 'Sorry, Dad'. Roberts praised his son's soldierly bearing throughout the ordeal, and the boy's schoolmates wrote that they had not realised they had such a hero in their midst. There's an intriguing loose press cutting in the rear of Roberts' 1918 diary discussing the anxiety of soldiers' young brothers approaching enlistment age as the war dragged remorselessly on.[24]

John's anxieties about Frank's enlistment, embarkation and service also help explain his response to his death. Frank's enlistment was compelled by family status and social pressure. Despite his fervent public patriotism, Roberts discouraged Frank's enlistment in July 1915, suggesting (19 July) that 'he should make inquiries from the authorities as to the need of farmers enlisting before doing so' and sending him, armed with his business card, to consult influential figures in defence and government circles who said (20 July) that Frank 'was not needed'. But Frank found that his young uncles, nephews and Dandenong neighbours, including his sweetheart's brother, were enlisting or preparing to enlist, so he followed in February 1916, at the age of 27. He entered officer training and did not embark until May 1917, by which time he had married and his wife was pregnant. Frank was so emotionally fraught when the time came to leave home and embark that his father discouraged the women from seeing him off. Roberts, who had superintended his son's every move at home, was able (using contacts) to subvert the tight security and track Frank's voyage to Britain. Frank underwent further officer training in England, but never served as an officer after he finally arrived in France in November 1917. His daughter was born that month, and Frank was killed just 10 months later.

Frank's attitude to army life varied according to whom he was writing – his uncle, his wife, or his father. Like most diggers he complained about the rations and the weather, of course, but he also expressed a venomous and merciless hatred for the enemy ('the German hogs'), and wrote home how impressed he was by the English officer who explained how to use the bayonet on Germans who made perfect targets when they threw down their weapons and raised their arms. Frank became an expert 'ratter' of enemy bodies, dead and living, and it is possible that some Germans lived only because Frank found it easier to rob a standing man than a prone one. His letter telling his infant daughter (not yet a year old) how proud she would be of her brave father might be excusable if it were not followed in his father's scrapbook by a family photograph (and not the only one) looted from the body of a German soldier. Despite his reluctance to enlist, Frank had contempt for the slackers at home: 'By God, sweetie,' he wrote to Ruby, 'I wouldn't be a slacker who has to look the men of Australia in the face when we march home. I consider myself a man, Darl, I've faced death with the fine lads of Aussie ... God damn all white livered cowards.' He wanted the war prosecuted to the end: 'My dear girl, we don't *want* peace yet, because we ... we want to give [the Hun] a taste of *war in his own country*, then he'll lie down like a whipped cur'. Foolish bravado, perhaps, but his letters testify to the coarsening, even brutalising, impact of war service.[25] His last letter to his wife, however, suggested that Frank had something of an epiphany. He had seen too much dying to be fearful; he now only cared for those who would be left. This Australian infantryman had foreseen his death.

Frank as the archetypal Digger: from man to superman

What Frank's descendants made of these diaries, letters and scrapbooks in succeeding decades is uncertain. John Roberts' state of chronic depression appears to have lifted from the mid-1920s, when he ceased placing annual in memoriam notices in the press. He had intended writing a book, but it never eventuated. Peter Stanley suggests he may have lost faith in the claims made for the significance of the battle of Mont St Quentin. This seems

Charles Web Gilbert's clay model for the bronze statue for the 2nd Division AIF memorial at Mont St Quentin, France, stood at 13 feet six inches, and was completed at his Fitzroy studio in 1922. J.G. Roberts papers, State Library Victoria, YMS 8508, Scrapbook No. 7, folio 246.

unlikely: Frank's grave at Peronne was visited in 1919 by Australia's greatest general, John Monash (Roberts was acquainted with Monash's daughter, who accompanied her father to France), and there was a photograph to prove it; Roberts devoured Monash's bestseller *The Australian Victories in France 1918* extolling the battle; and a large and very lifelike diorama of the battle of Mont St Quentin graced the Australian War Museum in Melbourne when it opened fully in Melbourne's Exhibition Building on Anzac Day 1922.[26] (Frank's little daughter, four-year-old Nancy, became distressed when she saw the display, calling for her Daddy.) Above all there was the massive 13' 6'' sculpture that from 1925 stood atop the 2nd Division memorial in France, of a Digger trammelling and bayonetting a struggling German eagle. When John's friend the sculptor C. Web Gilbert wanted to model the Digger on Frank, John readily agreed, writing in his diary on 7 February 1919 that 'as Frank appears to have lost his life when attacking with the bayonet the design suits his ending very well'. Gilbert told a reporter that 'It is my task to create a superman'.[27] The Digger's face was taken from a photograph of Frank but modelled in life at the Fitzroy studio by his young brother Bert.[28] 'Gilbert,' Roberts noted in his diary (25 January 1922), 'said ... Sir John Monash had been greatly impressed with the Mont St Quentin figure'. To Monash, it seems, this figure represented the archetypal Digger.[29]

On Anzac Day 1929 journalist Bob Croll published this tribute to Frank:

> he was ... a true Digger. His very gravestone testifies to the fact, for on it are cut the words from one of the last letters he wrote: 'Not lonely with the boys; I'm one of the Aussie family here.' ... Justly did his friend Web Gilbert take Frank Roberts for his model ... His clear cut features and lean, well-knit body may rightly be regarded as representing the Australia type ever, as his keen resourceful mind typified the 'digger' spirit.[30]

So it is quite mistaken of Tanja Luckins to suggest that Roberts was embittered by the war and by Frank's death, and 'wondered whether the war had been worth it'.[31] He denounced anti-conscriptionists as traitors to the fighting men, the nation and the Empire, and criticised Prime Minister Hughes for failing to enforce conscription in 1917 without a vote. He was among the crowds who welcomed home the nation's conquering heroes in 1919: on Saturday morning 30 August he left his city office to hail 'Prime Minister Billy Hughes on his return from England, the Peace Conference in Paris etc etc a wonderful reception', and on Boxing Day he 'lined up with other members present of the Sailors and Soldiers Fathers' Association to welcome Lieut Genl Sir John Monash late Commander of the Australian Imperial Force in France. Had a handshake from him'.

On 11 November 1919, the first silent observance of the armistice, 'during [the] 2 minutes stoppage I thought as well of Frank as of other brave boys I knew or whose parents I knew, who had died in the War'. The accountant in him just had to count them: 'there were over 40'. At lunchtime he met his brother Will, and in the evening – no doubt with his scissors at hand – he read the *Saturday Evening Post.* When he cast his vote in the December 13 Federal election he clipped from a newspaper the Victorian Protestant Association's voting ticket warning against what it termed the 'Mannix-Ryan ticket', and afterwards stuck it into his diary. He remained a fervent Imperial patriot, proudly showing visitors his memorial volumes to Frank. In 1922 he began another scrapbook, this time of the Royal Visit of the Prince of Wales, who came to thank Australia for its part in the Great War. In his diary he noted his, Berta and Gwen's sightings of the prince, though he did not divulge whether Gwen had danced with a man who had danced with a girl who had danced with HRH.

With the national celebration of Anzac Day, Gallipoli came to eclipse the achievements of the AIF in France. But John Roberts died early in 1933, before the world slid toward another war after Hitler came to power that year, before in 1940 the invading German army destroyed the offensive statue atop the Mont St Quentin memorial, and before the appearance in 1942, just after the Japanese attack in the Pacific, of the final volume of

CEW Bean's history of the first AIF. Frank's name had finally appeared in a book – as a footnote.[32]

Bruce Scates thought John Roberts' 'elaborate grief ... a comment on power and privilege'.[33] It also testified to the power of Australia's middle class to generate legends they could live by. Bill Gammage and Joan Beaumont have written, memorably, of the Australian soldiers' *Broken Years* and of our *Broken Nation*. John Roberts perhaps exemplified the broken-hearted but stiff upper-lipped folk who peopled the Commonwealth after 'the war to end all wars'.

Notes

1 John Garibaldi Roberts' diary for 1921 opens 'My 43rd Diary'. His diaries for 1915–1921 are in the La Trobe Manuscripts Collection at State Library Victoria: SLV MSS.MS 5782 Box 265/1-4 [1915–1918], MS 9105 Box 266/1-2 [1919–1920], and MS 5786, Box 266/3 [1921]. Dr Bart Ziino kindly alerted me to Roberts' 1922 diary, which is held in the Alfred Deakin Prime Ministerial Library, Special Collections, Deakin University Library, Geelong.

2 Pat Jalland, *Changing Ways of Death in Twentieth Century Australia: War, Medicine and the Funeral Business* (Sydney: NSW Press, 2006), 377, describes the diaries as 'one of the few such detailed sources left by grieving families'.

3 Thomas Mallon, *A Book of One's Own: People and Their Diaries* (New York: Ticknor & Fields, 1984), xvi–xvii.

4 Katie Holmes, *Spaces in Her Day: Australian Women's Diaries 1920s–1930s* (Sydney: Allen & Unwin, 1985), xv.

5 Mallon, *A Book of One's Own*, xvii.

6 'A Peace of Justice,' *Argus*, 25 June 1919, 9.

7 See the entries for John Garibaldi Roberts and William Joshua Roberts in volume 11 of the *Australian Dictionary of Biography*.

8 Joy Damousi, *The Labour of Loss: Mourning, Memory and Wartime Bereavement in Australia* (Melbourne: Cambridge University Press, 1999); Pat Jalland, *Australian Ways of Death: A Social and Cultural History 1840–1918* (Melbourne: Oxford University Press, 2002); Pat Jalland, *Changing Ways of Death in Twentieth Century Australia: War, Medicine and the Funeral Business* (Sydney: UNSW Press, 2006); Tanja Luckins, *The Gates of Memory: Australian People's Experiences and Memories of Loss and the Great War* (Fremantle: Curtin University Books, 2004); Peter Stanley, *Men of Mont St Quentin: between victory and death* (Melbourne: Scribe Publications, 2009).

9 Jalland, *Australian Ways of Death*, 320.

10 Stanley's account ('Prologue', *Men of Mont St Quentin,* 1–5) begins 'Roberts rose early' (for which there is no evidence), and tells us that Roberta and her young son were already at 'Sunnyside' (Roberts wrote that they 'left for Sunnyside this morning'), that 'the postman delivered a letter from Frank [that Roberts] shared ... with Gwen' (when it was a letter *for* Gwen that she shared with her father), and that he telephoned his in-laws with the awful news (when his brother Will undertook this). Such mistakes may seem pettifogging, but they nevertheless betray inattention to detail.

11 Luckins, 19.

12 Diary, 13 September 1918 (but actually written on 18 September).

13 The 1918 railways timetable (in effect from 6 May that year), and kindly supplied by Len Regan of the Australian Timetable Association, reveals John's circumscribed travel options on Friday 13 November. The earlier (1 pm from Flinders Street) train would have delivered him to Upper Fern Tree Gully for a long walk to Belgrave and then on to 'Sunnyside', and in his business suit and shoes.

14 *Herald,* 23 September 1918, pasted in Roberts' diary, with corrections in ink.

15 In 1933, however, his graveside service was conducted by the Rev. Canon Sutton of Holy Trinity, Kew, a friend of Will Roberts: *Herald,* 14 February 1933, 11.

16 Luckins, 40–1: 'A break in his diary routine is evident, as there are changes in the page layout of the diary'; 'changes to his manner of diary-keeping'; 'a new form ... that reveals the depth of his grief'. Actually, Roberts' diary, after a narrative of the six days 13–18 September (not dissimilar from the narrative of his young son's accident earlier in the year), quickly resumes what Luckins terms its 'matter-of-fact' character.

17 Luckins, 43. If anyone receives more attention in John's diary, it is his remaining son Bert, whose health and schooling preoccupy his father.

18 'Fascinating Library,' *Herald,* 5 Aug 1920, 11. Other accounts: *The New Idea,* 6 July 1905; 'Knowledge in the Hills / An Amazing Home-made Encyclopedia,' *Argus*, 25 April 1931; and ' "Dad – Of Dandenong Range" / Foster Father of Artists,' *The Age,* 18 May 1929.

19 Kevin Molloy, 'From Kallista to Mont St Quentin', *The La Trobe Journal,* No. 98 (September 2016): 135. John Lack consulted seven key volumes.

20 Kevin Molloy ('From Kallista to Mont St Quentin') is the first historian to discuss the challenge of reconstructing and interpreting Roberts' intentions.

21 Not far removed from the style of Blackadder's 'Algernon was not long on Gallipoli before he formed the distinct impression that someone was trying to kill him'.

22 Letters contained in J.G. Roberts, Scrapbook 7: SLV MS 8508, folios 40–61, and the diary as cited.

23 Accounts and letters in Roberts' Scrapbook No. 7.

24 Diary entry 28–29 January 1918, a pasted-in section demonstrating, *contra* Luckins, that this practice did not begin with Frank's death; and 'Fathers and Sons: Men Before Their Time', *The Leader,* 3 August 1918.

25 Extracts from Frank's letters pasted into John Roberts' diary, 1 September 1919.

26 David Dunstan, 'A Mecca for Australians', in David Dunstan, *Victorian Icon: The Royal Exhibition Building* (Melbourne: Australian Scholarly Publishing, Melbourne 1996), 328–33.

27 *Herald,* 6 August 1921, 11.

28 Many references in Roberts' 1922 diary.

29 See also Monash quoted in 'How Mont St Quentin Was Won: A New Way of Telling a Battle Story,' *Pals: An Australian Paper for Boys,* 22 April 1922, 823–4: cutting in Roberts Scrapbook No. 7, at folio 245.

30 R.H. Croll, 'Hated war but not afraid to fight,' *Sun News-Pictorial,* 25 April 1929. Peter Stanley suggests that this may have been written as the foreword to John Roberts' projected book.

31 Luckins, 47, 133.

32 C.E.W. Bean, *The Australian Imperial Force in France during the Allied Offensive, 1918* (Melbourne: Angus and Robertson, 1942), 844, footnote 25.

33 Bruce Scates, *Return to Gallipoli: Walking the Battlefields of the Great War* (Melbourne: Cambridge University Press, 2006), 17.

Forewarned, Forearmed

Australia and the Spanish Influenza Pandemic, 1918–1919

ANTHEA HYSLOP

In the latter months of the Great War, a lethal strain of influenza wrought global havoc, infecting around a third of the world's population and killing some fifty millions at least. Like other countries, Australia suffered huge disruption and unprecedented mortality; but its relative remoteness and island isolation made possible a system of strict maritime quarantine, which delayed influenza's entry into the community until early 1919, enabling preparations to be made, while the virus itself became less aggressive. In New Zealand, Spanish influenza had entered unchecked with disastrous results. By contrast, Australia's pandemic was milder, although still a traumatic ordeal.

***

The pandemic influenza of 1918–1919 first became prevalent in the United States in the northern spring of 1918, where it broke out among soldiers in military camps. From there it was carried aboard troopships to Europe and its battlefields, where it caused widespread sickness. It then travelled around the globe, reaching Australia and New Zealand by September of that year. In this first wave, the disease appeared somewhat severe, but not alarmingly so. However, by August of 1918 the influenza virus in western Europe had undergone a dramatic change, becoming far more deadly, with rapid onset and a marked increase in pneumonic complications. In the worst cases, victims' lungs filled with a bloody froth, causing a 'heliotrope' cyanosis that darkened the skin as death approached. Mortality was highest among men and women in the prime of life, rather than in infants and the elderly, who were usually most vulnerable to 'flu'. This second wave of influenza, and after it a third wave, killed many millions around the world in the last months of the Great War. The global total of deaths is now thought to have been at least fifty million, perhaps as many as one hundred million. And the death toll was highest in less-developed countries, notably in India and many parts of Africa.[1]

By late October 1918, the new strain of 'flu' was wreaking havoc in South Africa and New Zealand, and both those countries grimly warned Australia that the only effective measure was to prevent its entry. A cable from New Zealand's health authorities declared:

> Can safely say true influenza type has been replaced by pneumonic and septicaemic types: preferably call it epidemic pneumonia: epidemic spreads just as quickly as people move from place to place by tram or train or motor: mortality is appalling: treatment by vaccine utterly futile once this epidemic is started: no attempt made here to give prophylactic vaccine because insufficient medical and nursing aid available for either step and infinitely too slow to catch up with speed of spreading: only effective measure your side will be to prevent introduction of epidemic pneumonia into Australia.[2]

Australia's maritime quarantine system had already been reinforced by specific measures against influenza, and these were now intensified. Any vessel coming from either South Africa or New Zealand, whether infected or not, would be quarantined for seven days unless the ship's master could declare that there had been no shore contact. Shipping from other places, if 'clean' for the previous two weeks, would spend three days in quarantine or seven days if not 'clean'. Any vessel carrying influenza would be isolated until its outbreak was controlled. Sick passengers and crew would be sent to the quarantine station's hospital, while the healthy remained on board to undergo vaccination with a bacterial vaccine, daily temperature parades, and daily inhalations of a 1 or 2 per cent zinc sulphate spray.[3]

Maritime quarantine, depending as it did on accurate medical records, correct diagnosis, and the integrity of ships' masters, was not expected to contain the disease indefinitely. Yet, remarkably, it managed to waylay the 'flu' for almost three months. During that time over one hundred vessels, including troopships of returning soldiers, underwent the quarantine process, mostly at Sydney's North Head but also at other major ports around the country. This breathing space gave government authorities at all levels more time to prepare for the pandemic's onslaught. Plans were made for closing schools and places of public resort, banning public meetings, setting up vaccination depots and emergency hospitals, organising medical, nursing and ambulance services, and issuing health advice to the public. In November 1918, federal and state leaders met to co-ordinate a national response and agreed to adopt a system whereby those states as yet free of infection would close their borders against an infected neighbour until they too became infected. Dr JHL (Howard) Cumpston, Australia's Director-General of Quarantine, doubted that closing land borders would work, but the states insisted on it. In addition, the federal authorities would control both land and sea traffic in an infected state, but it was up to that state to notify them of its plight. Popularly called 'Spanish 'flu', the disease would be officially termed 'pneumonic influenza'.[4]

Meanwhile, at the coastal quarantine stations, thousands of returning soldiers and civilian travellers were passing through maritime quarantine. Troopships returning home from Europe were usually free of 'flu' by the time they reached Australia, but a few had only just set out *for* Europe when peace was declared, and therefore returned home after a much shorter voyage. The *Boonah* had left Fremantle on 30 October 1918, with 164 crew and 931 troops from several states bound for France. Arriving at Durban,

South Africa a few days after the Armistice, the ship was turned back, despite its captain's best efforts, but not before influenza had got aboard. By the time the *Boonah* reached Fremantle on 11 December, there had been 298 cases. The sick were taken to Woodman Point, there to be nursed by twenty nurses from another troopship, the *Wyreema*, who had volunteered their services. Twenty-four of the men and four of the nurses died of influenza. Those still aboard the *Boonah* then had to endure weeks of delay, first at Perth then at Albany, and last at Adelaide, by which time 'flu' was beginning to appear in Melbourne.[5]

Another troopship, the *Medic*, with 156 crew and 829 troops aboard, had been making for Europe via Panama when recalled by the Armistice. On the way home it called at Wellington, New Zealand to refuel, and picked up influenza as well. By the time the *Medic* reached Sydney on 21 November, there were 203 cases and twelve had died.[6] A senior quarantine officer who boarded the vessel described the troops' plight:

> The scene on board was remarkable. A score or more of stalwart young men lay helpless about the after well-deck awaiting transport to the improvised and overflowing hospitals in the troop-decks. That they lay there was not due to any neglect or delay on the part of the busy stretcher-bearers, but to the extraordinarily sudden and disabling onset of the disease. One smart, well set-up young soldier came up a companion-ladder close to where I stood, held on for a few seconds to a rail, and then sagged slowly down till he assumed the characteristic, flattened sprawl on deck. There was no pretence or 'old-soldiering' about it. The men were being literally knocked down by a profound systematic intoxication of extraordinarily rapid onset.[7]

In quarantine at North Head, a further 112 men from the *Medic* fell sick and another ten died, together with two Army nurses. One of those nurses was Annie Egan. Aged twenty-seven and a Roman Catholic, her plea to see a priest before her death on 5 December had to be refused, in keeping with quarantine rules. This caused outrage and a sectarian furore in Sydney, with an indignant Archbishop Kelly calling it 'an impious refusal'. Like other Army personnel who died there, Nurse Egan was buried with full military honours at North Head. A few weeks later, arrangements were made for a priest to enter North Head, provided quarantine requirements were met.[8]

Eventually, in early January 1919, just when it seemed as if Australia as a whole would be spared, Spanish influenza did make its way into the community – *not* in Sydney, where maritime quarantine was busiest, but in Melbourne, at that time the seat of Australia's federal government. Exactly how it got in remains unclear but it probably evaded, rather than broke out of, quarantine since no breach could be discovered. Macfarlane Burnet's surmise, put forward in 1942, that a single 'undetected carrier' without symptoms could have taken the 'flu' from quarantine into the community would explain, firstly, why there was no recorded breach of quarantine before the disease appeared in Melbourne, and next, why there was no immediate explosive spread of cases, as had occurred in other countries.[9]

By 22 January 1919 the Melbourne Hospital's Medical Superintendent, Dr RP McMeekin, was reporting numerous cases of 'influenzal pneumonia'. Several of the case were fatal, and McMeekin stated his own belief that an epidemic disease, similar to if not identical with Spanish influenza, was spreading rapidly. Federal and Victorian health authorities promptly conferred together, but concluded that, as this disease seemed to lack both Spanish influenza's explosive infectivity and the 'intense toxaemia' seen in the quarantine stations, the evidence so far did not warrant Victoria's declaration as an infected state.[10] Alas, only a day or so before Dr McMeekin's warning, the disease was already making its way by train from Melbourne to Sydney. A returning soldier found himself sharing a compartment with a very sick civilian, and two days later was himself admitted to the military hospital at Randwick.[11] There, the rapid spread of influenza among those attending him left the New South Wales government in no doubt, and on 27 January a cable to Melbourne announced that New South Wales, albeit with only a score or so of cases, was an infected state. An embarrassed

Victoria, by now with over 350 cases, hastily reviewed its situation and declared itself infected next day.[12]

For a time, chaos reigned between federal and state governments. New South Wales promptly closed its borders against Victoria, even though *both* states were now infected. All the other states took similar action, and also imposed their own maritime restrictions, even more rigorous than the Commonwealth's. Interstate cargo shipping was seriously disrupted, and island Tasmania virtually severed its links with the mainland for months.[13] Queensland and Western Australia caused interstate trains to be halted at their borders, and all passengers underwent a period of quarantine in primitive conditions. At Tenterfield in northern New South Wales, hundreds of Queensland holiday-makers, returning from Sydney with depleted funds, had to find lodgings where they could, until a tent city was set up at the local showgrounds. This was followed by another encampment at Wallangarra on the Queensland side of the border.[14] At Parkeston in Western Australia, passengers on the halted Transcontinental train had to sleep on board in hot, dusty conditions while they served a week's quarantine. After three unpleasant days, earth closets were provided, but a large marquee erected for leisure use was blown away by a sandstorm.[15] South Australia likewise halted passengers from Victoria and New South Wales to keep out fresh cases of influenza, despite the state's having been declared infected on 4 February.[16]

At first, most states had to cope without their premiers who had been attending a national meeting in Melbourne and were now marooned there, except for New South Wales whose premier had prudently returned to Sydney by special train on 25 January. Angry cables sped to and fro as Dr Cumpston rebuked the states for excessive zeal, while the states charged both Victorian and federal authorities with selfish negligence.[17] By 6 February this dissension, and the states' recalcitrance, had resulted in the abandonment of November's federal agreement.[18] Meanwhile, influenza spread rapidly in Victoria and New South Wales, entering South Australia a week later, and Queensland by early May. But border quarantine, though chaotic at first, did indeed slow influenza's progress around the country, and those states infected last, Western Australia and Tasmania, did experience a milder epidemic.

Despite the spread of 'flu', Dr Cumpston for his part remained unconvinced that the disease in the community was the same as that in the quarantine stations. As a precaution, therefore, he insisted on keeping federal maritime quarantine measures in place, until late April 1919.[19] This, by the way, negates a British author's recent assertion that the pandemic entered Australia because quarantine had been lifted 'too soon'.[20] It is worth adding here that a major breach of quarantine did occur at Sydney's North Head, but this took place in early February, by which time Spanish 'flu' had already arrived in Sydney from Melbourne. After many delays, the troopship *Argyllshire* had reached Sydney on 9 February, having picked up an extra soldier in Melbourne, who promptly developed 'flu'-like symptoms. This sent the ship into quarantine at North Head. Two days later, some 900 uninfected soldiers from the *Argyllshire*, objecting to primitive accommodation in snake-infested scrubland, proceeded in orderly fashion first to Manly where they were put on a ferry, and subsequently marched through the city wearing facemasks, to the Sydney Cricket Ground, where they completed their term of quarantine.[21]

Everywhere, as Spanish influenza spread, state schools, community halls and other public buildings were pressed into service as emergency hospitals. In Melbourne, chief among these was the Exhibition Building which could accommodate at least 1,500 patients on iron bedsteads in its vast halls. With capacity limited at first by staffing shortages, Victoria's government welcomed an offer from Roman Catholic Archbishop Mannix to staff the hospital with unpaid nursing nuns and members of teaching orders whose schools were closed. This, however, aroused indignation among the hospital's existing nurses who apparently had not been consulted. It also provoked a sectarian outburst from the Reverend Henry Worrall, a prominent Methodist, against what he called 'the enormity' of placing mostly Protestant patients in the care of 'a sacerdotally trained band of anti-Protestants' whose garb, customs and ceremonies, he declared, 'should not be introduced into a State hospital'. Seeking to pacify all parties, the state government now proposed that the religious orders should staff another emergency hospital instead. But Mannix called this 'a weak surrender to sectarianism' and in high dudgeon withdrew his offer.[22] Clearly, the resentments of the wartime conscription debates were quick to resurface under stress. Nonetheless, and despite its rather rugged accommodation, the Exhibition Hospital continued to function until the epidemic's end, treating over 4,000 cases in total and with a death rate of just under ten percent, comparable to that in Melbourne's established hospitals.[23]

Transfer of the sick to emergency hospitals was compulsory at first, and efforts were made to isolate 'contacts' also. Later, home isolation was preferred where possible; stricken households signalled their need by placing a yellow flag or a warning notice in a window and teams of volunteers were organised to render assistance. Meanwhile, schools were closed, theatres and cinemas likewise, and race meetings and other public gatherings cancelled. The wearing of facemasks in public was widely adopted and was even compulsory for a time in New South Wales. Municipal inhalation chambers were set up to provide 'internal fumigation' by means of inhaling an antiseptic spray, a process that became quite popular with the public. And many thousands of people received injections of a bacterial vaccine; most were given at public vaccination centres, free of charge, some from their own doctor for a small fee.[24]

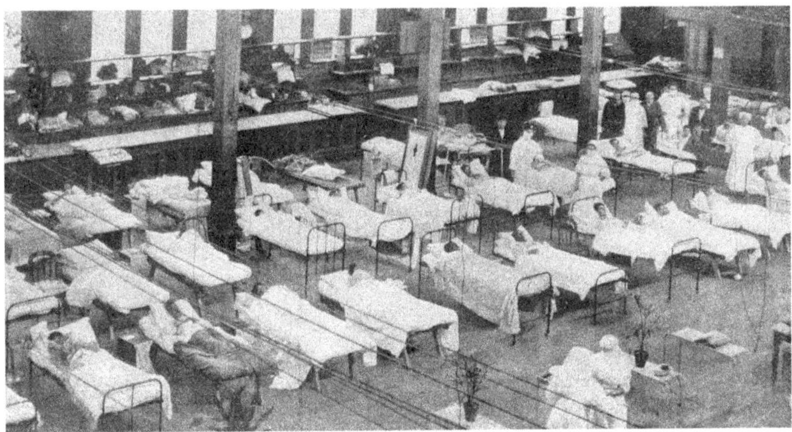

Influenza victims at the Melbourne Exhibition Building. *Sydney Mail,* 19 February 1919.

In 1918, bacteriology was at the forefront of medical science, and researchers were only beginning to realise the existence of 'filter-passers', known today as viruses. Influenza was believed to be a bacterial disease and, as the pandemic took hold, bacteriologists in countries like Britain and the United States worked frantically to develop bacterial vaccines that might prevent it, or at least diminish its severity. Their efforts appear to have been of some benefit, but were hampered by dire circumstances and the impossibility of meeting a sudden, huge public demand.[25] In New Zealand, Spanish influenza's impact was so massive that a vaccination scheme could not be attempted. By contrast, in Australia the success of maritime quarantine gave health authorities a unique opportunity to test the efficacy of 'protective inoculation'. By mid-October 1918, many weeks before influenza entered the community, a bacterial vaccine was being produced at the new Commonwealth Serum Laboratories in Melbourne, for use in quarantine stations and by the public.

The Commonwealth Serum Laboratories (CSL) had been founded only three years earlier, in response to wartime demand for bacteriological materials and advances in the control and prevention of infectious diseases. With Dr William Penfold as its first Director, the CSL began work in Melbourne in early 1917, moving into specially designed premises at Royal Park in July 1918.[26] Barely three months later, all its resources were devoted to producing and distributing influenza vaccine, some three million doses of it in the six months to mid-March 1919 alone. For its preparation, several organisms isolated in the sputum or post-mortem material of influenza cases in quarantine, were grown in various media and combined into a bacterial 'cocktail' to be administered in two successive doses. At first, bacillus influenzae ('Pfeiffer's bacillus') had not been isolated, but by December the first or 'A strength' dose of one c.c. contained the following: bacillus influenzae, 25 millions (m) per c.c.; micrococcus catarrhalis, 25 m; pneumococcus, 10 m; streptococcus, 10 m; and another gram-positive diplococcus, 10 m. The second or 'B strength' dose, to be administered a week later, was likewise of one c.c. but five times stronger.[27] In later years, this bacterial vaccine was derided as useless, because influenza is a viral disease. Yet, despite its limitations, it seemed to confer some protection, if not from pneumonic influenza itself, at least from its more severe complications. Statistical analyses made at the time clearly linked inoculation with a diminished case mortality.[28]

Most of Australia's medical profession approved of the vaccine, and some used it to treat patients already ill with influenza in order to reduce complications. Other doctors advocated special remedies of their own, such as daily hot baths, or injections of a mercury solution to reduce high fever. However, medical treatment in general was 'symptomatic': they required doses of expectorant, inhalations, cold compresses for headache, purges if needed, aspirin for fever and pain. Severe cases in hospital might require digitalis with strychnine for a feeble pulse, or aspiration to draw off fluid from the lungs. There was much comparing of notes on influenza therapies in the weekly issues of the *Medical Journal of Australia*.[29] The general public, for their part, also favoured home cures involving onions or camphor, alcoholic drinks, especially whisky, and patent cold remedies, such as Hearne's Bronchitis Cure, Bosisto's 'Parrot Brand' Eucalyptus Oil, or Wawn's Wonder Wool. Aspirin, in the form of Nicholas's Aspro, carried a 'flu' sufferer's testimonial: 'The doctor told me it would shift it out of me in 24 hours and he was right'. Other patent products made preventive claims: Greathead's Mixture, an antiseptic mouthwash, would 'prevent contagion'; Clement's Tonic would 'purify the blood'; Curenza, a nasal ointment, was allegedly 'checking the disease in Sydney'; Dr Morse's Indian Root Pills were 'a searching, cleansing remedy'. Most of these products were used as short-term substitutes for orthodox medicine, and their makers invariably recommended going to bed and calling the doctor at the first sign of 'flu' symptoms. In the community at large, great admiration was expressed for the doctors and nurses who risked their lives, and sometimes lost them, in the service of others during the pandemic.[30]

Of a population of around five million, it was at first thought that at least twelve thousand Australians had died of pneumonic influenza: some as soldiers, still overseas or on returning troopships, a few in remote areas far from help, many in quarantine stations, most in isolation hospitals or at home. That total however, was conservative, and the figure is now thought to have been well over fourteen thousand.[31] Yet even so, the relative mildness of Australia's experience is made clear by comparison with neighbouring New Zealand, where Spanish influenza, entering and spreading unchecked late in 1918, took more than eight thousand lives in a population of just over one million.[32] Here in Australia, the mortality rate was higher in those states first infected: in Victoria 243 per 100,000; in New South Wales 304 per 100,000. It was lower in those states infected later: in Tasmania, 114 per 100,000.[33] The pandemic's impact on Australia's indigenous population was not well recorded at the time, and still is not fully told. However, it is nonetheless clear that the indigenous death toll was heavy indeed, much more so than that of the rest of the population. This matches the experience of New Zealand, where over two thousand Maori died of influenza, a mortality of 42.3 per thousand of their own people. This was some seven times higher than the European death rate. In both instances, the chief causes appear to have been the poor conditions in under-resourced reservations or settlements and a lack of immunity to introduced disease.[34]

Australia's influenza ordeal lasted longer than most but was less severe. The disease's virulence had waned somewhat, first in quarantine, then in its delayed progress around the country. Widespread use of a bacterial vaccine, albeit a rather blunt weapon, probably saved lives also. Today, Australians know that, with much faster international travel, their geographic isolation can no longer be relied on to fend off another such pandemic. But today also, an international monitoring network keeps influenza under close and constant observation. Since the 1940s, modern virology has been producing increasingly effective vaccines to keep up with the volatile influenza virus in all its varied manifestations. For all that, this country's management of a future pandemic may well still depend as much as it did in 1919 on household quarantine, municipal delivery of relief, community cooperation and the work of volunteers.

Spanish influenza caused severe stress and great hardship wherever it went. In Australia, state and federal governments were in bitter dispute for several months. Trade and business were seriously hampered, travel was impeded, industrial unrest broke out on waterfronts, livelihoods were threatened and all manner of activities suspended for a time. As the pandemic waned, so too did the tension and disruption, and life returned to normal for most. But for families stricken by sudden illness and death it would never be the same. And it is doubtless for this reason that Spanish influenza, half-forgotten for much of the twentieth century, was remembered longest, preserved in family lore, by those who themselves or whose forebears had suffered grievous loss: the pandemic's most lasting impact.

Notes

1 For accounts of the pandemic's global impact see: Alfred W. Crosby, *America's Forgotten Pandemic. The Influenza of 1918* (Cambridge: Cambridge University Press, 1989); Geoffrey W. Rice, *Black November. The 1918 influenza pandemic in New Zealand* (Christchurch: Canterbury University Press, 2nd edn., 2005); Howard Phillips, *'Black October': the Impact of the Spanish Influenza Pandemic of 1918 on South Africa* (Pretoria: Government Printer, 1990); Niall Johnson, *Britain and the 1918–19 Influenza Pandemic. A dark epilogue* (Routledge: Abingdon, 2006). The global estimate of deaths is that cited by Johnson, 77–81.

2 Quoted in JHL Cumpston, *The Health of the People. A study in federalism* (Roebuck: Canberra, 1978), 34–5.

3 The system is outlined in JHL Cumpston, *Influenza and Maritime Quarantine in Australia*, Commonwealth of Australia Quarantine Service Publication No. 18 (Melbourne: Government Printer, 1919), 7–11. Its operation is detailed in subsequent chapters.

4 Commonwealth and States of Australia Influenza Conference 1918. Resolutions (undated typescript, Australian Archives (AA): series A2, item 1919/482, pt 2.) See also Cumpston, 63–6; Anthea Hyslop, 'Insidious Immigrant: Spanish Influenza and Border Quarantine in Australia 1919', in *From Migration to Mining. Medicine and Health in Australian History*, ed. Suzanne Parry (Darwin: Historical Society of the Northern Territory, 1998), 201–15. The disease is thought to have been called 'Spanish' because in Spain, a non-combatant country, news of its impact was unfettered by wartime censorship.

5 Cumpston, 139–41. For a full account of the *Boonah*'s story, see Ian Darroch, *The Boonah Tragedy* (Bassendean: Access Press, 2004).

6 Cumpston, 23 and *passim* in ch. IV. See also Jean Duncan Foley, *In Quarantine. A*

History of Sydney's Quarantine Station 1828–1984 (Sydney: Kangaroo Press, 1995), 110–12.

7 Cumpston quotes the officer on 53, calling him normally 'unimpressionable'.

8 Duncan Foley, *In Quarantine*, 113–14.

9 F.M. Burnet and Ellen Clark, *Influenza. A survey of the last 50 years in the light of modern work on the virus of epidemic influenza*, Walter & Eliza Hall Institute Monograph No. 4 (Melbourne: Macmillan, 1942), 101. Chapters VI and VII of this work present a detailed analysis of the 1918–19 pandemic.

10 *Argus*, 23, 24 January 1919; *The Age*, 23, 24 January 1919; Minute, 23 January 1919, from Cumpston to Comptroller-General (Customs), Prime Minister's Department: Influenza – Victoria. Declaration of Infected Area (AA, series A2, item 1919/742).

11 W.G. Armstrong, *Report on the Influenza Pandemic in New South Wales in 1919* (Section V of *Report of the Director-General of Public Health, New South Wales, for the year 1919*, Sydney: Government Printer, *NSWPP* 1920, Vol.1), Part I, 'Epidemiology and Administration', 148–9.

12 *Argus*, 28, 29 January 1919. For a close study of January 1919 events in Melbourne, and Cumpston's role therein, see Anthea Hyslop, 'A Question of Identity: JHL Cumpston and Spanish Influenza, 1918–1919', in *Intellect and Emotion: Essays in Honour of Michael Roe*, eds David Walker and Michael Bennet (*Australian Cultural History*, No. 16, 1997/98), 60–76.

13 Prime Minister's Department, Files of Papers: Influenza Epidemic. Commonwealth Regulations, c. 2 February 1919 (AA: series A6006, item 1919/2/3); *Sydney Morning Herald*, 31 January 1919. See also: Cumpston, *Health of the People*, 34–40; Hyslop, 'Insidious Immigrant', 205–7.

14 *Warwick Examiner & Times*, 29 January 1919; *Warwick Daily News*, 1, 5, 8 February 1919; *Queensland Times*, 1–19 February, 1–12 March 1919; *Brisbane Courier*, 1, 5 February 1919; *Sydney Morning Herald*, 15 February 1919.

15 *West Australian*, 5–8, 11 February 1919; Report of CA Stephens, Acting DC Supervisor, to Superintendent, Port Augusta, 6 February 1919 (AA: series A2, item 19/1311); Hon. J Mackinnon Fowler to WA Watt, 7 February 1919 (AA: series A2, item 19/1131).

16 Premier, SA, telegram to Acting PM, 5 February 1919 (AA: series A2, item 1919/993).

17 Influenza. Commonwealth Regulations, c. 2 February 1919; also attached memorandum initialled by WA Watt; Correspondence, between various state premiers and Acting PM Watt (AA: series A2, item 1919/1302), early February 1919. (See Hyslop, 'Insidious Immigrant', for full details of these.)

18 *Argus*, 6 February 1919; *Sydney Morning Herald*, 29 January, 8 February 1919; *Brisbane Courier*, 7 February 1919; *West Australian*, 11 February 1919.

19 *Argus*, 29 January 1919; *Sydney Morning Herald*, 29 January 1919; Cumpston, 52, 62.

20 Laura Spinney, *Pale Rider. The Spanish Flu of 1918 and How it Changed the World* (Vintage: London, 2017), 44. Spinney cites no source for this statement.

21 *Argus*, 12 February 1919, *Sydney Morning Herald*, 12 February 1919; Duncan Foley, *In Quarantine*, 114–15.

22 *Argus*, 5, 11, 15, 17, 18, 21 February 1919; *The Age*, February and March 1919; *Advocate* (Melbourne), 22 February, 1, 8 March 1919; *No-Popery and the Spanish Influenza*, Australian Catholic Truth Society pamphlet, 1919.

23 For an account of the Exhibition Building's role in 1919, see Anthea Hyslop, 'Fever Hospital' in *Victorian Icon. The Royal Exhibition Building, Melbourne*, ed. David Dunstan (Melbourne: The Exhibition Trustees, 1996), 320–7.

24 Armstrong, *Report on the Influenza Pandemic*, Part I, 157–64. The measures taken in other states were similar to those described by Armstrong for NSW.

25 Crosby, *The Forgotten Pandemic*, 84, 100–1; Johnson, *Britain and the 1918–19 Influenza Pandemic*, 136, 143–5.

26 A.H. Brogan, *Committed to Saving Lives. A History of the Commonwealth Serum Laboratories* (Melbourne: Hyland House, 1919), 1–11.

27 W.J. Penfold, 'Influenza Vaccine and Inoculation': Ch. VII in Cumpston, *Influenza and Maritime Quarantine*, 73–88; Armstrong, Report on the Influenza Pandemic, Part I, 153–7; Brogan, *Committed to Saving Lives*, 12–18.

28 T.M. Cherry, 'The Value of Inoculation – A Statistical Inquiry', ch. VIII in Cumpston, 89–119.

29 *Medical Journal of Australia*, October 1918 to June 1919, *passim*. For details, see Anthea Hyslop, 'Old Ways, New Means: Fighting Spanish Influenza in Australia, 1918–1919', in *New Countries and Old Medicine. Proceedings of an International Conference on the History of Medicine and Health* (Auckland: Pyramid Press, 1994), eds Linda Bryder and Derek A. Dow (Auckland: Pyramid Press, 1995), 54–60.

30 Advertisements for patent medicines appeared plentifully in daily newspapers throughout the influenza epidemic. See for example *Argus*, *The Age*, *Sydney Morning Herald*. Details of home cures are recorded in letters sent by Australians in the early 1970s to Richard Collier, author of *The Plague of the Spanish Lady. The Influenza Pandemic of 1918–1919* (London: Macmillan, 1974). Collier's papers are now held in the Imperial War Museum, London.

31 J.H.L. Cumpston, *Health and Disease in Australia. A History*, intro. and ed. M.J. Lewis (Canberra: Australian Government Printing Service, 1989), 319; Johnson, *Britain and the 1918–19 Influenza Pandemic*, 81.

32 Rice, *Black November*, 18.

33 *Official Year Book of the Commonwealth of Australia, 1901–1919* (Melbourne: Government Printer, 1920), 1129.

34 See Gordon Briscoe, *Queensland Aborigines and the Spanish Influenza Pandemic of 1918–1919* (Canberra: AIATSIS, 1996); Rice, *Black November*, ch. 7.

Marie Stopes and the Banning of *Wise Parenthood*

FAY WOODHOUSE

As the playground rhyme had it:

Sister Susie built her hopes
On the book of Marie Stopes.
But I fear from her condition
She must have read the wrong edition.[1]

This paper explains why the pregnancy of any Australian Sister Susie would have been more likely the result of her being unable to obtain any edition of Stopes' book *Wise Parenthood*, which had been banned in 1923.

Fans of *Downton Abbey* will remember the scene in Series Five where Lady Mary Crawley asks her maid Anna to purchase a contraceptive device recommended by Dr Marie Stopes. The widowed Lady Mary was not about to let nature take its natural course. She intended to avoid any unintended consequences from her week's liaison with Lord Gillingham – the man she thought she wanted to marry. In her quest to acquire the Cervical Cap, Anna had to assure the female chemist that she was a married woman who did not want more children, and we were shown Anna pointing to a diagram in one of Marie Stopes' books. The scene ends with a very embarrassed Anna running from the shop with the device but leaving the instructions behind. When she relates the episode to Lady Mary, Anna realises how unfair it was. Buying the Cervical Cap was not a right; she was a working-class woman *and* she had to prove to the chemist that she did not want to have more children. Had Lady Mary gone to the chemist shop herself, she would not have had to prove anything.

Downton Abbey is a fictional family drama, but nevertheless it highlights the reality of strongly disapproving attitudes to contraception and birth control after the war. The same issues were prevalent in Australia in the inter-war years. In Australia, as in England, the rich and educated like Lady Mary could afford to purchase this type of contraceptive device, while working-class women like Anna had much less chance of managing their own birth control issues by this method.

Marie Stopes, born in 1880, was a British paleobotanist, author and campaigner for eugenics and women's rights. Stopes was the youngest person in Britain to earn a Doctor of Science from the University of London before studying the reproduction of living cycads at the University of Munich where she was awarded a Doctor of Philosophy in botany in 1904. She held the post of Lecturer in Paleobotany at the University of Manchester from 1904 to 1910 and also lectured at University College London. In 1913, after she began writing a book about the way she thought marriage should work, she met the American campaigner, Margaret Sanger who had coined the term 'birth control', and conferred with her on her chapter on contraception. As Jane Carey argues, Stopes and Sanger both promoted birth control as a eugenic tool; the two terms were intertwined, and even synonymous in this period. In the years after the war, Stopes and Sanger 'went on to spearhead remarkably similar campaigns for eugenic birth control, which were emulated by like-minded reformers in Australia'.[2] Marie Stopes' first book was rejected by numerous publishers, but once published it was an instant success.

Married Love: A New Contribution to the Solution of Sex Difficulties was published in 1918. It was dedicated to 'young husbands and all those who are betrothed in love'. Stopes had 'some things to say about sex, which so far as I am aware, have not yet been said'.[3] *Married Love* advocated that sexual happiness was the right of every man and woman. She writes that, 'particularly in the middle classes in this country, marriage is far less really happy than its surface appears.' Like her readers, Stopes had been brought up to be romantically idealistic and abysmally ignorant about sex.[4] Seen by one reviewer as a 'delightful and romantic essay on the married state', the language of the book was a product of its times. Euphemistic expressions allude to the nature of man's desire and the mystical and spiritual union of man and woman. While Stopes did not include any illustrations in *Married Love*, her clinically detached descriptions were clear, straightforward and no doubt ahead of their time. *Married Love* was advertised in the *Medical Journal of Australia* in December 1919, along with other recently released publications. Articles reviewing the book appeared in the Australian press in January, April, July, November and December 1919.[5] Reviews continued throughout 1920 and 1921. The Sydney *World's News* declared that the book was 'absolutely the most sensible we have met with on this subject, and we unhesitatingly recommend it to all those who are married, or on the eve of marriage'.[6] Stopes and her views were also criticised. The Brisbane *Daily Standard* in January 1921 objected to her 'view to lay the foundations of a new sexual code'; perceived promiscuity in marriage and a demand for easier divorce.[7]

Wise Parenthood: A Practical Sequel to 'Married Love': A Book for Married People[8] was published in late 1918 and a copy of it, dated 1919, is held at the State Library Victoria. Stopes presented *Wise Parenthood* as a 'treatise on Birth Control for married people'. It was written to answer the questions posed by readers of *Married Love* and to tell prospective parents 'how best to control the conception of desired children so as to space them in the way best adjusted to what health, wealth and happiness they have to give'. In her Introduction Stopes writes that 'The subject of the control of conception has not hitherto received the learned importance it deserves.'[9] Her book was reviewed by the *Medical Times* and the *Eugenics Review*. The *Eugenics Review* reviewer wrote that 'the practice of birth control is one of the few modern tendencies which the sociologist can regard with satisfaction... like contraception, her book was inevitable'. The *Medical Times* declared that 'the author ably presents the case for birth control from the scientific point of view'.[10] In 1920 the *Daily Express* quoted Stopes' summary of her work as 'A book for those creating the future', invoking eugenics philosophy.

In her teens Stopes had met Sir Francis Galton, the British anthropologist who coined the word 'eugenics' in 1883. Inspired by Darwin's evolutionary theory, and the idea of the 'survival of the fittest', it argued that human evolution could be advanced through selectively encouraging reproduction among 'superior' individuals. As Galton defined it, eugenics was 'all the influences that improve the inborn qualities of *a race*; also, those that develop them to the utmost advantage'.[11] Galton's views were also clearly racist. In the early twentieth century, eugenics enjoyed wide support amongst both conservatives and progressive reformers. Organised eugenics movements emerged in Germany, Britain, the United States and Australasia.[12] Marie Stopes believed in the principals of eugenics and saw birth control in that light. Jane Carey argues that her publications 'were not particularly eugenically oriented'. They do, however, provoke another understanding of the terms 'birth control' and 'contraception'. Today the two terms are used interchangeably to mean methods to stop conception.[13]

A book of only 62 pages, *Wise Parenthood* contains two illustrations; the first a diagram of the female reproductive organs, and the second drawings and descriptions of the Cervical Cap. It is thought that the presence of these diagrams may have been the cause for the banning of *Wise Parenthood* in Australia in 1923. What were the influences at play leading up to the banning of Marie Stopes' book in Australia?

In 1919 in post-war Australia, the Government faced significant social problems. The first was the falling birth-rate; the second was the increasing prevalence of venereal disease in Australia. The medical profession saw these problems as moral issues and blamed the falling birth rate largely on the availability of birth control literature and contraceptive devices. Not as much fuss was made of the increasing incidence of venereal disease and the dangers it posed to both mother and baby. The government and medical men saw the 'prevention of conception' as a frustration of natural law. Working class women in particular saw it differently. The churches, Protestant and Catholic, held strong opinions on the role of women; Victorian notions of innocence and purity prevailed and rested on the sanctity of the female body.[14] Motherhood was seen as a sacred duty. Yet the First World War had accelerated social change. As Janet McCalman points out, World War One had 'delivered knowledge of birth control down the class system and sexual licence up it'. People's sexual behaviour was different after the War.[15]

The falling birth rate in Australia

During the 1890s Australia experienced a 'spectacular decline' in the birth rate. By 1903 many prominent Australians feared that the decline was evidence of national decay comparable with that in France in the 1870s. In August 1903 the New South Wales government instigated a Royal Commission on the Decline of the Birth Rate under the chairmanship of Dr C.K. Mackellar. Its purpose was to investigate the causes 'which have contributed to the decline of the birth rate in NSW and the effects of the restriction of child-bearing upon the well-being of the community'.[16] It was the world's first such inquiry. Historian Neville Hicks studied the debate around the falling birth rate and the Commission's subsequent report. He writes that the 'statistical evidence for the decline in population growth was daunting'. From 1891 until 1900 net migration decreased and there was an uninterrupted downward trend in the average rate of natural increase. As with migration, the years around the turn of the century saw a major shift away from the pattern of growth experienced in the boom years of the 1880s. The *Report* found that between 1891 and 1911 the average size of completed families fell from 7.03 to 5.25.[17] Most of the overall decline in the birth rate was caused by a reduction of fertility within marriage.

What was evident to the Commissioners was the effect of the deliberate limitation of fertility being practised by the women of Australia. Hicks argues that the Mackellar Commission 'began with firm assumptions about the evidence for, and the causes of, the matters into which they were inquiring', and that they directed the responses of their witnesses towards confirmation of these assumptions. Their discoveries about contraception and abortion practices was considered so scandalous, that strenuous attempts were made to suppress the Commission's final *Report*. Completed in 1904, it reflected a conservative response to the changing social climate believed to be responsible for the increased use of contraception.[18] Copies sent to the Secretary of State for the Colonies disappeared without trace and even the Commissioners who wrote the *Report* found it hard to access a copy. Doctors, clergymen, politicians, editors and many others already worried by the implications of the declining birth rate were seriously disturbed by the Royal Commission's findings.[19] The *Report* also concluded that 'the possibility of maintaining a "white Australia" depended on ... whether Australia was capable of maintaining a large population'. The falling birth rate was addressed by restricting, (effectively banning) information about how to prevent pregnancy, and to define such information as obscene, and so illegal and therefore censored.[20] The Commission also recommended an increased emphasis by the clergy on the teaching of correct moral attitudes.[21]

In response to the *Report*, the poet and writer, Dame Mary Gilmore, argued in *The Worker* that 'religious leaders holding up their hands in horror at the empty cradles – would do better to pay attention to the empty cupboards'.[22] Similarly, Rose Scott, an early feminist, denounced the findings as 'a Commission composed of men, a Report in which the only evidence was as these men approved of, [and] a Commission which was very contentedly assuring the public that everything was the fault of the women'.[23] Historian Deana Heath links the censorship of birth control literature to Australia's anxiety about the viability of the white population and the White Australia Policy.[24] This theory is convincing.

The medical profession's view

The 'menace' of the low birth-rate was addressed by Professor Richard Berry in December 1917. As President of the Victorian Branch of the British Medical Association he cited Professor Karl Pearson's study of Britain's falling birth rate. Pearson, also a eugenicist, was the first Galton Chair of Eugenics at London University. His report appears to have influenced Berry's thinking.

Part of the study was written by Miss Ethel M Elderton, Galton Fellow of the University of London. Elderton questioned whether the fall in the birth rate was due to natural causes or to the deliberate limitation of the family, and what part changing social and economic conditions played. In examining the statistics, the report noted that in each region examined in the study, increased education had aided the limitation of the family. Pearson posited the view that 'the menace of the birth-rate' was 'a question on which the whole future of our race depends'.[25] In his 1917 address published in the *Medical Journal of Australia,* Berry was clearly disturbed by these findings. He concluded his article by reiterating the words of the Pearson-Elderton report: 'the decline was taking place in almost every part of the British Empire ... including Australia'.[26]

Berry's article prompted vigorous debate in the *Journal* throughout 1918 and 1919. In January 1918, James Booth and 'Pater Familias' responded to the Pearson report and Berry's interpretation of it. Booth proposed that, 'the married woman has a right to have time for her own development, and if we are wise we shall see that she has it'.[27] 'Pater Familias' argued that the menace of the birth-rate was largely an economic question, and asked his colleagues: 'How many medical men in Australia have families of more than four children in each? It would be interesting to know ... I considered four children were as many as I could afford to provide for'.[28] Dr J Rosenthal proposed that another reason for the drop in the birth rate was the fear of childbirth: 'It is the horror of the agonizing pain endured at the first childbirth, which makes some women terrified at the thought of going through with it again. I have spoken to several women who have only had one child, and it is the same tale over and over again.'[29] The Federal Council of the British Medical Association published its report in the 24 August edition of the *Medical Journal of Australia*.[30] It acknowledged that the dangers of venereal disease, euphemistically known as the 'red plague', miscarriages and inadequate child welfare were contributing factors to the falling birth-rate. The author emphasized therefore that the duty of medical practitioners was to make their patients and the public aware of the effect of venereal diseases in bringing about sterility and miscarriage.[31] Gynaecologists had already warned that the return of thousands of 'grossly infected soldiers' would do untold damage to the women and to the nation, 'robbing women of their health and the nation of their potential babies'.[32]

The dangers of sexually transmitted diseases were also addressed by progressive Christians and health reformers alike. Published medical reports prompted the State President of the Women's Christian Temperance Union (WCTU) to declare that:

> We, as women, have ever refused to discuss the awful question of impurity, but it has crept steadily on until today the red plague is not only a menace to the young of the country, but if it is not dealt with, [will] become a national scourge.[33]

Stopes was so concerned about venereal disease that she wrote about its dangers, in *Truth about Venereal Disease* (1921).[34] Despite their warnings, it appears governments ignored the problem of venereal disease and chose to target and blame women alone for the falling birth rate. The attitude adopted by governments illustrates the hypocrisy and double standards in play during the 1920s.

In *Sex and Suffering: women's health and a women's hospital*, Janet McCalman notes that in the late nineteenth century and the first decades of the twentieth century, medical training did not include a study of contraception or birth control. In her study of childbirth at the Royal Women's Hospital she reveals that medical trainees sent out to the slums of Fitzroy were sometimes asked by husbands for contraceptive advice before they examined or delivered the babies. McCalman notes that one doctor, when asked to give a few hints on contraception, reported that 'Not knowing any, I couldn't enlighten him'.[35]

The impact of the First World War on men and women was significant. As McCalman writes, women felt freer and more independent, and by the 1920s they began to look different. The new fashions helped; dresses with shorter hems and simpler styles using less fabric could be made with paper patterns and a cheap sewing machine at home.[36] The 'new woman' with new expectations of life, love and marriage, looked and behaved in a very different way from her mother and grandmother.

As McCalman observed, family limitation began when women decided they had enough children and began preventing pregnancy. One inexpensive method available to working-class women was the Higginson syringe for douching after intercourse. Sold by the Women's Hospital, chemists and birth control campaigners, it was widely available and was found in thousands of Australian homes. Occasional intercourse reduced the chances of conception and the 'once-a-month' or 'once-a-fortnight' rule inevitably meant women stopped having children. To achieve this result, despite the fact that the menstrual cycle was not fully understood until the 1920s, is itself remarkable. For many couples, complete abstinence was 'unhappily common': women were tired, unwell and cross, and had 'had enough'. After having given birth to large numbers of children, instead of sex, their men were then expected to find consolation in 'beer and betting'.[37] Finally, induced abortion was a widely used birth control practice. Drugs were available, were advertised in newspapers and were sold by chemists everywhere. While some doctors performed safe terminations, they were liable to be charged because abortion was a crime at the time. The poor also sought the help of the midwife who 'knew about such things'.[38] Combined, these methods did influence the falling birth rate among the working class.

The attitude of the churches

The churches, Protestant and Catholic, retained their view that a woman's sacred role was to bear children.[39] The traditional view of the Catholic Church was that the primary purpose of marital sex was procreation. Sex was sinful except when it occurred between married couples, and artificial contraception was against the 'natural law'.[40] The Protestant churches held differing views. In 1908 the Lambeth Conference of the Anglican Church stated that birth control 'cannot be spoken of without repugnance' and denounced it as 'demoralising ... and hostile to national welfare'. The Conference recorded with alarm the growing practice of the artificial restriction of the family, and earnestly called upon all Christians to 'reject the use of artificial means of restriction' as hostile to national welfare.[41]

While the church hierarchy maintained the status quo, reformers in Protestant churches emerged. The Women's Christian Temperance Union [WCTU], the Young Women's Christian Association [YWCA] and the Mothers' Union became political lobbyists between the 1890s and the 1930s, promoting social reform and moral issues grounded in 'family values'. Ellen Warne's history of these organisations, *Agitate, Educate, Organise, Legislate*, explores the ways they targeted a wide range of issues including the growing sexualisation of youth, with particular focus on birth control and sex education, discussed as 'sex hygiene'. Members of these groups waged public campaigns to establish sex education, especially in schools. Sadly, this did not happen until at least the 1940s. Still, they believed they had to 'replace the silence about sex within polite society' with 'well-informed facts about the functioning of the body's reproductive processes and the spread of sexually transmitted diseases'.[42]

The Women's Christian Temperance Union in particular saw women's suffrage as 'a right unjustly withheld'. Through attempts to expand the right of women to influence the male political sphere, members of the Union showed a remarkable eagerness to convince the public that traditional structures of gender and politics could bend to accommodate new forms of active, female citizenship.[43] The WCTU also successfully fought a campaign to change legislation to raise the age of consent from 12 to 16 so that very young girls could not consent to their own downfall. They saw the matter as one of 'vital importance to our sex and our nation ... [because] ... we dare no longer to ignore it'.[44] The WCTU, YMCA and the Mothers' Union campaigned vigorously that while in the past 'silence around sex had been the norm, it should not continue'. Modesty and embarrassment were no excuse according to one Mrs Harris who wrote that daughters not only needed to know, it was a daughter's right 'to expect instruction'. It was 'an actual sin', she concluded, 'if not a crime against children ... to reach marriageable age unprepared for the duties of the future'.[45] The arguments continued to be proposed by the women's groups but by the 1930s appear to have run their course.

The banning of Marie Stopes' books

In 1901 when the new federal *Customs Act* came into being, it largely focused on the censorship of blasphemous, indecent, and seditious publications being imported into Australia. The role of centralised federal censorship was strengthened by the introduction of military censorship during the First World War under the *War Precautions Act (1915)*. By the 1920s, Customs had established a national system of censorship administration which allowed officials to examine and ban imported material on the wharf, and to open and seize publications sent internationally by post. Publications falling into the category of 'blasphemous, indecent or obscene works or articles, or literature unduly emphasising matters of sex' were dealt with under Section 52 (c) of the *Customs Act*, or Item 14A of the Customs (Prohibited Imports) Regulations. There is little discussion about venereal disease in the Australian censor's records. Although Justice Windeyer's 1888 judgement declared that birth control literature was not obscene, historian Nicole Moore's study of censorship in Australia, *The Censor's Library*, indicates otherwise. Windeyer's judgement was often ignored and there was a pervasive tendency to class birth control literature as obscene.

In addition, Moore found that non-professional, cheap and easily accessible publications that appealed to the large market of working-class women were targeted by the censors and banned.[46]

Stefania Seidlecky and Diana Wyndham in *Populate and Perish*,[47] suggest that Marie Stopes' *Married Love* was banned for a time but that Customs allowed *Wise Parenthood.* This is contrary to my findings. On 24 May 1923, the Melbourne *Age* reported that *Wise Parenthood* had been banned by the censor. Articles reporting the ban appeared in newspapers from one end of Australia to the other. Articles questioning the decision included: 'An Absurd Censorship', 'Service to the Race', 'Minister calls for Report' and 'Should Dr Marie Stopes's Works be Banned?'. Others were published in letters to newspaper editors and in editorials throughout May and June 1923. The number of letters indicates the strong views held by the community. Most wrote in favour of the publication of *Wise Parenthood* although a few were against it. In Brisbane *The Worker* criticised the official responsible for imposing the a ban and cited a similar ban imposed in New Zealand where, she or he wrote, the banning of Dr Stopes's book 'was greeted with a chorus of derision and amusement in scientific circles and elsewhere'.[48] This was a common view of the banning. Correspondence from 'Gossip' declared simply: 'I wish I could write a book that was worth banning'! Articles on Marie Stopes and her work continued to be published in Australian newspapers throughout 1924 and 1925.

Conclusion

It is unclear why the ban on the sale of Marie Stopes' book *Wise Parenthood* was lifted in 1923. Although only a small sample of letters is quoted on this subject, they indicate that public pressure may have had considerable bearing on the case. The Comptroller of Customs reversed his decision and was convinced to allow the importation of *Wise Parenthood, Radiant Motherhood* and seven sexology and birth control titles. These included *Courtship and Marriage* by Thomas Hearne, *Marriage and Birth Control* by Brenda Barwon, *Wedded Love or Married Misery*, by W.N. Willis, and *Sexual Science as Applied to the Control of Motherhood* by J.P. Gair and *Love Ethics* by John Hurstcot.[49] Two editions of Stopes' book are held at The University of Melbourne BioMedical Library. The first is the 1921 edition, the second the 1923 edition. Copies are also held in the State and National Libraries.

How do we explain the banning in 1923 of *Wise Parenthood*, the second of Marie Stopes' books on marriage, sex, motherhood, birth control and contraception? It appears to have been a combination of the prevailing forces at the time rather than one specific cause. The churches, especially after the Great War, impressed upon women of all classes that their role was to breed. The government remained concerned by the consistently low birth rate in Australia. From 1901, the Australian government's desire was to achieve a white Australian population. It is noted that, throughout the debate on the falling birth rate and the arguments against birth control and contraception, the Aboriginal people were not considered.

Were these the motivating factors behind the Comptroller General's decision to ban this book? It was easier for middle-class women to purchase contraceptive devices (such as the Cervical Cap suggested by Marie Stopes) than it was for working-class women who frequently bore more children than they desired. In this way, banning books on contraception deprived them of achieving smaller families and happier, more confident sex lives. It might also ensure a steady increase in the birth rate . Whatever the rationale behind the banning, it remains clear that by the time the book was banned, enough people had read or purchased the book to respond with an outcry and to call out the Comptroller's actions as ill-conceived and misplaced. Marie Stopes' work remained in print until the 1960s and her methods remain as valid today as they were in 1918 and 1919.

Notes

1 Stefania Siedlecky & Diana Wyndham, *Populate and Perish: Australian Women's Fight for Birth Control* (Sydney: Allen & Unwin, 1990), 15.

2 Jane Carey, 'The Racial Imperatives of Sex: birth control and eugenics in Britain, the United States and Australia in the interwar years', *Women's History Review*, Vol. 21, No. 5, November 2012, 733–4.

3 Marie Carmichael Stopes, *Married Love: A New Contribution to the Solution of Sex Difficulties* (London: Putnam, 1918), xiv and 1.

4 June Rose, *Marie Stopes and the Sexual Revolution* (London: Faber and Faber, 1991), 112.

5 January (*Sydney Morning Herald*), April (*Hobart World*), July (*Hobart World*), November (Melbourne *Argus*) and December 1919 (Sydney *Stock and Station Journal*).

6 'Have You Read?', *World's News*, Sydney, 10 January 1920, 29.

7 'Married Love Dr Stopes Criticised', *Daily Standard*, Brisbane, 29 January 1921, 3.

8 Marie Carmichael Stopes, *Wise Parenthood A Sequel to Married Love* (London: Putnum, 1919, 12th edn., 1926), vii and 3.

9 *Wise Parenthood*, vi.

10 Ibid., 59.

11 Carey, 737; Keith Briant, *Marie Stopes A Biography* (London: The Hogarth Press, 1962), 31.

12 Carey, 737.

13 Ibid., 738.

14 Ellen Warne, *Agitate, Educate, Organise, Legislate* (Carlton: Melbourne University Publishing, 2017), 97.

15 Janet McCalman, *Sex and suffering: women's health and a women's hospital: the Royal Women's Hospital, Melbourne, 1856–1996* (Carlton: Melbourne University Press, 1998), 153–4.

16 Neville Hicks, *This Sin and Scandal: Australia's Population Debate 1891–1911* (Canberra: ANU Press, 1978), xv.

17 Hicks, *This Sin and Scandal*, xv–xvi.

18 Ibid., xvii.

19 Ibid., xvi.

20 *Populate and Perish*, 18; and Deana Heath 'Literary Censorship, Imperialism and the White Australia Policy', in *A History Book of the Book in Australia 1891–1945: A National Culture in A Colonial Market*. Eds. Martyn Lyons and John Arnold (St Lucia: University of Queensland Press, 2001), 69–82 quoted in Nicole Moore, *The Censor's Library* (St Lucia: University of Queensland Press, 2012), 43, 160–1.

21 Moore, *The Censor's Library*, 19.

22 Ibid.

23 Ibid.

24 Heath, quoted in Moore, 41.

25 R.J.A. Berry, 'The Menace of the Birth-Rate', *Medical Journal of Australia*, Vol. II, No. 24, 15 December 1917, 492.

26 Berry, 'The Menace of the Birth-Rate', 495.

27 James Booth, 'The Menace of the Birth-Rate', *Medical Journal of Australia,* 12 January 1918, 39.

28 'Pater Familias', 'The Menace of the Birth-Rate', *Medical Journal of Australia,* 26 January 1918, 80.

29 J. Rosenthal, 'The Menace of the Birth-Rate', *Medical Journal of Australia,* 19 January 1918, 59.

30 'Decline of the Birth-Rate in Australia', *Medical Journal of Australia,* 24 August 1918, 169.

31 'The Falling Birth-Rate', *Medical Journal of Australia,* 14 September 1918, 226.

32 McCalman, *Sex and suffering,* 152.

33 Warne, *Agitate, Educate, Organise, Legislate,* 103–4.

34 Marie Carmichael Stopes, *Truth About Venereal Disease* (London: Putnam, 1921).

35 McCalman, *Sex and suffering,* 186.

36 Ibid., 153.

37 Ibid., 126.

38 Ibid., 128.

39 Warne, *Agitate, Educate, Organise, Legislate,* 97.

40 Siedlecky & Wyndham, *Populate and Perish,* 15.

41 From 1930, the Anglican church permitted contraception under certain specified? circumstances. BBC – Religious – Christianity: Contraception, https://www.bbc.co.uk/religion/religions/christianity/christianethics/contraception_1.shtml, accessed 13 July 2019.

42 Warne, *Agitate, Educate, Organise, Legislate,* 93, 94.

43 Ibid., 5.

44 Ibid., 93, 97.

45 Ibid., 104.

46 Moore, *The Censor's Library,* 28–42.

47 Ibid., 41.

48 'Banned Books Dr Marie Stopes Falls Foul of Customs Officials', *The Worker,* Brisbane, 7 June 1923, 19.

49 Moore, *The Censor's Library,* 47.

The 1919 Inkstand Incident

Managing returned soldiers in Melbourne

ROSS MCMULLIN

With the Great War over at last, General Sir John Monash was placed in charge of repatriating around 160,000 Australian soldiers. Despite the shortage of available ships and other daunting difficulties, he applied his masterly administrative proficiency to this challenging task and carried it out with outstanding success. Appropriate criteria were established to determine which men were entitled to return sooner rather than later; the requisite ships were obtained from the British authorities; and the AIF did not experience the serious unrest that plagued the forces of some other countries during the immediate aftermath period.

Almost 77,000 soldiers (and 600 nurses) returned to Victoria in 1919, many more than had returned during the four years of war. That this was accomplished so effectively was a relief to the authorities, but they sensed they were not out of the woods. The adjustment of all these returning soldiers to civilian life could well prove a fraught process. The transition for many thousands of them was likely to be anything but straightforward after years of battlefield brutalities had scarred them irretrievably. They were returning with their severe physical and psychological legacies to a society transformed by the conflict. The bitterly contested conscription plebiscites had divided Australia profoundly, and the economy was still not in good shape: the cost of living had risen, the national debt had soared, industrial unrest was widespread, and there were not enough jobs. As well, the Spanish influenza pandemic was a lethal incursion. How readily the returned soldiers would adjust to a postwar existence in this fractured nation was uncertain. In fact, the prospect of unsettled diggers out of control generated considerable apprehension and, in some high-placed quarters, pronounced anxiety. Conservative powerbrokers were particularly perturbed. They were politically ascendant under the Nationalist Party banner following the seismic ALP schism of 1916–17. For these Nationalists, the possibility that war veterans might involve themselves alongside radical agitators in disruptive behaviour – perhaps even violent unrest – was nightmarish. If, however, the returned soldiers could be so harnessed or conditioned that most of them supported the Nationalists most of the time, they could prove an invaluable asset both politically and socially.[1]

J.F. Henderson, a former mayor of Essendon, identified one of his friends as just the man to guide and inspire returned soldiers on desirable lines. The friend was none other than Brigadier-General Harold 'Pompey' Elliott, the AIF's most famous fighting general. Henderson told Elliott that his role could well be crucial:

> Some one is needed to help direct the energies of the returned soldiers organisations, and I know of no one who appears to have such a hold on the affections of the men as you have, or whose advice they would be more likely to accept. The soldiers will of course be in a position to rule this country for some years to come if their energies are consolidated.[2]

Influential conservatives were pulling out all stops to orchestrate the type of soldiers' transition they wanted. Various groups had emerged to represent ex-servicemen and their interests, but the federal Nationalist government had come to a significant agreement with the most conservative of these organisations, the Returned Sailors and Soldiers' Imperial League of Australia (RSSILA, which was to become well known as the RSL). By granting the League 'official' status, the government provided it with invaluable patronage and disadvantaged rival associations. In return, the League's leaders privately assured senior Nationalists they would do their utmost to curb disruptive activities by returned soldiers and would 'avoid tactics which might embarrass the government'.[3]

Various incidents had intensified the conservatives' concern. There had been a number of unsettling events involving returned soldiers – mutinous shipboard incidents, a major riot in Adelaide, mayhem in Brisbane streets. Moreover, when the Nationalist premier of Western Australia led strikebreaking labour to Fremantle in order to smash a wharf labourers' strike in May 1919, it was a particularly alarming development for the authorities when they found that returning soldiers aboard a passing troopship proved more than willing to come to the aid of the strikers. The most insidious episode, however, occurred in mid-1919 in Melbourne.

The signing of the Versailles peace treaty in June 1919 was commemorated around Australia and beyond on 'Peace Day', Saturday 19 July. Celebrating the formal conclusion of such a terrible war was perfectly understandable, but it was an incongruous date for Australian jubilation. Few of those revelling in the celebrations realised that the date of the victory march was the third anniversary of the Western Front disaster of Fromelles, which remains the worst 24 hours in Australian history since European settlement. There were no fewer than 5,533 Australian casualties in a single night at Fromelles in a monstrously botched enterprise that resulted in no gain whatsoever. Wartime censorship had ensured that hardly anyone was aware of the magnitude of the calamity – apart from the survivors of Fromelles and their families.

Pompey Elliott's brigade had been slaughtered at Fromelles. He had foreseen that the ineptly conceived operation would prove a disaster, had resorted to unorthodox means to have it cancelled – unsuccessfully – and when it became the catastrophe he had predicted he then had to cope with the consequences. After the battle he was in anguish, 'tears streaming down

Pompey Elliott. Australian War Memorial, H15596.

his face' as he greeted shocked returning survivors and reiterated that the fiasco was not his fault.[4] What happened at Fromelles seared his soul and shortened his life.

So 19 July was hardly an appropriate date for Australians to celebrate victory, but in Melbourne – then the nation's capital – the crowd was large and the mood was joyful as 7,000 sailors and soldiers marched through the city. Afterwards, though, high spirits led to boisterousness, rebelliousness and arrests. Some returned soldiers resented what they regarded as excessive police heavy-handedness. They decided to raid Victoria Barracks in order to release some of the prisoners. In the ensuing skirmish one of the raiders, James O'Connor, was killed.

O'Connor was a labourer from Allansford who had been orphaned when only eighteen months old. He had volunteered early in the war but had been rejected because of his diminutive stature – he was less than five feet three inches tall and weighed less than nine stone. By 1916, however, recruitment standards were less rigorous and he was accepted; now eighteen and with no relatives, he named his employer as next-of-kin. O'Connor joined the 22nd Battalion at the Somme, where he was severely wounded in February 1917. His left thumb and index finger were blown off, and he ended up with bomb wounds to both legs, both hands, his face, left eye, left arm and scrotum. After two operations he was sent home, only to be fatally wounded in a different skirmish at Victoria Barracks.

The RSSILA convened an urgent meeting on Monday 21 July to discuss the recent events in Melbourne. The upshot was the dispatch of a deputation forthwith to the Police Commissioner, Sir George Steward. The delegation outlined their grievances about police conduct, and Steward agreed to investigate them. When the deputation returned to report to the RSSILA, however, the meeting was in no mood to be fobbed off by the prospect of some inquiry. They deserved better after fighting for their country and enduring the Western Front. Majority sentiment demanded immediate redress. Thousands of demonstrators proceeded to police headquarters. They found Steward in no mood to back down. He had agreed to look into their grievances, and he was not going to kowtow to an unruly mob.

Unable to obtain satisfaction from the police chief, the soldiers decided they should go higher still. They resolved to take their demands directly to the government of Victoria. So they made their way without delay to the state parliamentary offices. The premier of Victoria in 1919 was Harry Lawson, a Castlemaine lawyer in charge of a conservative government; honourable and courteous, pragmatic and experienced, he had been in the Victorian parliament for twenty years, having been first elected at the age of twenty-four.[5] He was presiding over a cabinet meeting when the soldiers arrived, but they did not let that deter them and burst in anyway to deliver their demands. They insisted on the dismissal of an especially loathed senior constable (J.E. Scanlon), an end to the wielding of police batons against returned servicemen, and the release of soldiers arrested during the weekend, together with remission of their fines.

Lawson urged the intruders to listen to reason and to uphold law and order. The leading dissidents refused to be mollified unless he acceded to their demands straightaway. His unwillingness to do so was in the circumstances tantamount to flourishing a red towel at these militant bulls. Amid extraordinary scenes of escalating disorder, offices were invaded, documents were ransacked, furniture was damaged, and an inkstand was hurled at Lawson, striking him heavily on the head. Shocked, dazed and with a deep gash on his left temple, he was guided away, trying to staunch with his handkerchief the blood that was already 'saturating his collar'.[6] The police were urgently summoned. A contingent arrived to disperse the insurgents. This proved no easy task. The police only managed to quell the invaders after resorting to a baton charge. Afterwards a violent melee erupted outside police headquarters. Various participants, both protesters and policemen, ended up in hospital. There were further clashes the following day.

The sequence of events, particularly the culminating violence against the head of an elected government, was profoundly disturbing. The returned soldiers had genuine complaints, and may have been influenced by non-AIF agitators, but the conservatives' worst nightmares about rampaging warriors had become real. Similar unruliness in Brisbane could be characterised as well-intentioned attempts to deal with dastardly 'Bolsheviks' and their 'disloyalist' acolytes who had infiltrated a radical Labor government up north, but in Melbourne a conservative premier was nursing a sore head and an acute grievance against the RSSILA after a demonstration under its auspices had resulted in intruders assaulting him in his government's offices. Corrective intervention was clearly necessary. Renowned military commanders were assembled to provide it. The State Commandant, Brigadier-General C.H. 'Digger' Brand, convened a mass meeting of returned soldiers at the Melbourne Domain on Wednesday 23 July. Thousands attended. They heard some of the best-known Melbourne-based leaders deliver a series of pep-talks on the need to curb disorderliness. Pompey Elliott was among the speakers, together with five other generals and three colonels.

Chairing the meeting was a 28-year-old manager, Gil Dyett. A Bendigo blacksmith's son, Dyett had served under Pompey Elliott at Gallipoli, where he had arrived in June 1915 with the fifth batch of reinforcements for Elliott's 7th Battalion. Shortly before the August offensive was due to begin, Dyett happened to receive an appetising array of preserved fruit and other delicacies from Egypt. He invited two other lieutenants from Bendigo, Noel Edwards and 'Curly' Symons, to join him in consuming them. All three admitted to feeling this would be their last meal; they would 'never see dear old Bendigo again'.[7] Their battalion entered the fray at Lone Pine soon afterwards. Symons, who was sent to a critical position by Pompey Elliott with a vigorous exhortation ('I don't expect to see you again, but we must not lose that post!'),[8] had a series of miraculous escapes and was awarded the Victoria Cross; Edwards was killed after displaying such conspicuous gallantry that those with him felt he too should have been awarded the supreme decoration; Dyett was hit and gravely wounded with numerous severe injuries including spinal damage. Deafened and concussed, Dyett was carried down to the beach, where his lifelessness resulted in a blanket being reverently placed over him prior to burial. Then someone noticed him move. During his protracted recuperation Dyett was told he would never walk again. But he recovered and was later able to list walking among his recreations. After returning home he involved himself in recruiting while remaining against conscription. He gained a reputation as an assiduous and effective organiser, and was elected the RSSILA's national president just eight days before chairing the important meeting at the Melbourne Domain. Dyett and Pompey Elliott had not seen each other for four years until July 1919. Now here they were together at this significant gathering, stepping up onto a waggon serving as an improvised platform to proclaim their abhorrence of unruliness.

Dyett opened proceedings and called on General Brand to speak. The purpose of the meeting was to 'restore the good name of the AIF', Brand declared, after recent events had tainted the army and the League with 'disgrace'. The only way to remedy the damage was for the 'law-abiding' returned soldiers to dissociate themselves from the 'disloyal element', who were dangerous 'hoodlums'. He added that Sir George Steward was 'a man of the world and a true friend of the Digger'.[9]

Pompey Elliott followed Brand, and his speech was influential. When Dyett introduced him he was given a rapturous reception. 'I want to say a few words about our conduct', Elliott began, associating himself with his audience right from the outset.[10] They had enlisted voluntarily to overcome a brand of tyranny that aspired to world domination, he pointed out, yet some returned men were now misguidedly associating themselves with forces of disorder tainted by not dissimilar tyranny. Attempting to coerce an elected government with threats and violence was unjustifiable, Elliott continued. Australia was a proud and free democracy, where rich and poor were equal before the law. Its soldiers should appreciate and uphold its system of government. If they did not approve of what a government was doing or not doing, their remedy was to vote against it on election day. He reminded them that 'money did not grow on trees, and the more damage that was inflicted by wanton outrages of the sort that had occurred during the last few days the less chance there was of the community giving aid to the soldiers who needed it'. While he valued his friendships with returned soldiers, 'it was impossible to remain friends with any man who deliberately associated himself with assaults on the heads of recognised governments'.

Elliott urged soldiers to show restraint, while empathising with their frustration that some returned men, 'through no fault of their own, were out of employment and were suffering hardship'. It was 'essential that we should not mix ourselves up in disturbances in the city', he declared. He added an astute analogy. In the 'battles we fought in together it was possible that there were many Germans who were opposed utterly to German militarism and despotism, but it was impossible for us to discriminate in a bayonet charge'. Similarly, even if mere curiosity prompted some returned men to join the crowds in Melbourne, it was equally 'impossible for those guarding the city to discriminate in carrying out their duty'.

The other speeches were in similar vein. Elliott's friend Brigadier-General Robert Smith reaffirmed that mob violence was abhorrent and the soldiers did not need to resort to it anyway, because they could control the democratic process via the ballot box through their votes and those of their families. Captain G.A. Burkett, a member of the Victorian RSSILA executive, concurred; he pointed out that the League 'had been battling for the rights of the soldiers' for months, 'but in one fell swoop nearly everything had been undone because a few of them went "stone mad" and wanted to smash things'. Lieutenant-Colonel H.E. Cohen urged the men to uphold 'law and order and the good name of the AIF. Nobody, he said, ever got any good out of blue metal and bottles'. There was, however, an AIF battalion commander who expressed a different view about violence at the Domain meeting:

> Lieutenant-Colonel Crowther declared that if there was to be a brawl in Melbourne by all means let there be one, but let them see that no decent fellow or any man with respect for the AIF was in it. If all decent men kept out of the brawls, the only people who would be hurt were the people who deserved it, and the sooner they got well hurt the better. (Laughter.)

After all the speeches had been delivered, Dyett brought the meeting to a significant culmination. He unequivocally condemned 'the shameless and lawless' assault on Premier Lawson – who was, as he knew from his recruiting activities, 'a true friend of the soldier'[11] – and then called on everyone present to raise an arm if they supported the maintenance of law and order. The response was unanimous, and highlighted by the newspapers. The *Argus* proclaimed it under multiple headlines – 'UPHOLDING THE LAW: SOLDIERS WILL AID: EMPHATIC DECLARATION'[12] – and *The Age* trumpeted it as a 'TRIUMPH FOR LAW AND ORDER'.[13] The Melbourne *Herald* reported that 'the Domain rang with the cheers which answered each appeal for good citizenship', and declared that the concluding resolution was a 'solemn pledge' that 'may become historic'.[14]

The ensuing decline in disorderliness in Melbourne indicates that this meeting (and the press coverage of it) was influential. Returned soldiers generally accepted that violence was an undesirable avenue to remedy grievances in a democratic society. The animosity and tension subsided. The streets became quiet. The sense of relief was fervent and widespread.

For the federal election five months later the Nationalists endorsed well-known AIF identities as Senate candidates in each mainland state except South Australia. They chose Pompey Elliott in Victoria, and he topped the Senate poll. Harry Lawson continued as premier of Victoria until 1924; when the notorious 1923 police strike exposed central Melbourne to mayhem, he relied on Monash and Elliott to organise a force of special constables – largely returned soldiers – to restore order.[15] Gil Dyett remained RSSILA president for 27 years.

Notes

1 Ross McMullin, *The Light on the Hill: The Australian Labor Party 1891–1991* (Melbourne: Oxford University Press, 1991), 117.

2 J.F. Henderson to H.E. Elliott 15 January 1919, Elliott papers 2DRL 513/43, Australian War Memorial, Canberra.

3 Marilyn Lake, *The Limits of Hope: Soldier Settlement in Victoria 1915–38* (Melbourne: Oxford University Press, 1987), 211.

4 Ross McMullin, *Pompey Elliott* (Melbourne: Scribe, 2002), 224.

5 Margaret Fitzherbert, 'Harry Lawson, sure and steady', in Paul Strangio and Brian Costar (eds), *The Victorian Premiers 1856–2006* (Sydney: The Federation Press, 2006), 161–70.

6 *Argus,* 22 July 1919; see also, for the events of 21 July, the evening paper, *Herald,* 21 July 1919, and *The Age,* 22 July 1919.

7 McMullin, *Pompey Elliott* (2002), 156.

8 Ross McMullin, *Pompey Elliott at War: In His Own Words* (Melbourne: Scribe, 2017), 79.

9 *Herald*, 23 July 1919.

10 This, and the following quotations from speeches given on 23 July, has been taken from *The Age,* 24 July 1919.

11 *Argus,* 24 July 1919.

12 Ibid.

13 *The Age*, 24 July 1919.

14 *Herald*, 23 July 1919.

15 McMullin, *Pompey Elliott* (2002), 586–90.

Maurice Blackburn and the 1919 Seamen's Strike in Australia

CAROLYN RASMUSSEN

One hundred years on, the year 1919 still holds the Australian record for the number of man-days lost (6,308,200) and wages foregone (£3,951,900) due to industrial conflict.[1] For that the Seamen's Strike, lasting from 9 May to 26 August, was largely responsible. The stoppage cost 2.7 million working days, and lasted longer than both the Maritime Strike of 1890 and the Great Strike of 1917.[2] And its impact was Australia-wide.

The armistice of November 1918 brought an end to the gunfire in faraway Europe, and was greeted in Australia with relief and jubilation, but it brought little healing to a home front still riven by the conscription imbroglios and by animosities generated by the Great Strike of 1917, and the outstanding question of equitable sharing of the war's economic cost. In addition, longer-standing divisions within the labour movement over the benefit or otherwise of the Conciliation and Arbitration system and, indeed, of putting Labor men into parliament, were unresolved and threatening to widen. Industrial relations were especially volatile on the waterfront, not only in Australia but around the world. The author's great-grand uncle was an active member of the far-left American Longshoremen's Union that instigated a General Strike in February 1919 by more than 65,000 workers

Maurice Blackburn. Courtesy of the Blackburn family.

on the western seaboard at Seattle. After two years of wartime controls, dissatisfied unionists stopped to gain higher wages. Although the strike was non-violent and lasted less than a week, government officials, the press, and much of the public viewed it as a radical attempt to subvert American institutions.[3]

In Australia, seamen as well as wharf labourers were also spoiling for some recompense for war-time hardships as well as a chance to use their industrial muscle, that is 'direct action' to challenge the power of the Conciliation and Arbitration Commission to reduce their bargaining power with employers. In his article 'Mr Justice Higgins Scuppered', an admirable account of the 1919 strike, Richard Morris focussed on the strikers' victory – the strike settlement and subsequent modifications to Arbitration law that rode rough-shod over the national wages policy enshrined in Arbitration Court determinations and precipitated a search by the Hughes Government for a renewed consensus on pay levels and the resignation of the President of the Court Mr Justice Higgins.[4] But the resolution of the drawn-out and costly conflict owed much to the efforts of recently defeated Labor member for Essendon, lawyer and Victorian Labor Party branch president, Maurice Blackburn, whom Morris overlooked. Nor do union histories, including one by Blackburn's devoted admirer Brian Fitzpatrick, accord him a role.[5] Maurice Blackburn has become the missing actor in the drama, and the resolution, of the Seamen's Strike of 1919.

Maurice Blackburn, educated at Melbourne Grammar School and the University of Melbourne and founder, in 1919, of the law firm that still bears his name, was 'converted' to socialism in 1904, and after a period in the Victorian Socialist Party he joined the Labor Party. Elected the member for Essendon in the Victorian Legislative Assembly in 1914, he lost the seat in 1917 as a consequence of his high-profile role in the campaign against conscription. He was re-elected to the Legislative Assembly in 1925 as the member for Fitzroy (afterwards Clifton Hill) in one of the more colourful elections in Victorian history, where he remained until 1933. Following a term as Speaker in the Legislative Assembly, he was elected to the federal seat of Bourke – covering Brunswick and Coburg – which he held until

1943. Counted among the left-wing of the Labor Party, he would be twice expelled for following his conscience, rather than its dictates – especially on matters of freedom of association and conscription – but his fine legal mind was at all times at the service of the Party and anyone suffering some form of injustice. A warm, affable man of simple tastes, but a fierce advocate, at the time of his death in 1944 at the age of 63 he had acquired a legendary status among his many followers.[6] Back in 1919 Blackburn was riding the crest of a wave that was taking him into deeply troubled waters.

Jim Scullin, later Prime Minister of Australia, handed over the presidency of the Victorian Branch of the ALP to Blackburn in April 1919, content 'that there was no man in the movement in any part of Australia for whom he would vacate the chair with greater pleasure'.[7] Blackburn's loss of his seat in the Victorian parliament in 1917 was a form of political martyrdom that had greatly enhanced his status inside a labour movement instinctively suspicious of a Melbourne-Grammar-educated lawyer. It also signalled a major setback for a party that had suffered a significant split. So it was that Blackburn assumed the presidency at a pivotal moment in the history of the labour movement as it faced dismal electoral prospects (except in Queensland), rising cost of living pressures, and accommodated the fall-out from the Bolshevik revolution in Russia.

If the war had not polarised the community enough, the revolution in Russia stoked fires of division that would smoulder for the next twenty years and beyond, occasionally flaring to white heat. The Bolshevik triumph provoked division within the labour movement almost as much as it gave fuel and energy to the conservative assault on that movement. Blackburn stood at a pivotal point in these divisions, finding himself on a number of occasions as a key broker or circuit breaker in the volatile atmosphere immediately following the war when it was unclear where on the political spectrum the labour movement might steady itself.

Blackburn's personal response to the Russian revolution was one of optimism and enthusiasm. His January 1919 pamphlet, *Bolshevism: What the Russian Workers are Doing*, was the first published in Australia in support of the revolution, but that did not mean he thought the Russian experience was one to be copied, anymore than the violence of the French Revolution was a model. 'Fortunately', in Australia, he argued, with its British heritage of previous 'sacrifice and struggle' against the sort of 'despotism that Russia [and France] had', there was no need to take such drastic action. He was confident that Australia would 'be able to make [her] own changes, peaceably, quietly and bloodlessly'.[8]

In the wider community the reverberations from the Bolshevik Revolution immediately altered the political and social climate. Whereas before 1917 socialists like Blackburn only had need to differentiate themselves from those theorists who preached the violent seizure of power, now they had to differentiate themselves from actual violent revolution. Furthermore, that violence had been made all the more reprehensible by the Bolshevik withdrawal of Russian troops from the Allied war effort. For patriots, already incensed by the labour movement's role in defeating conscription, this act of treachery recast any form of support for socialism as tantamount to treason. Emblematic of this changed mood was the Red Flag, the mere flying of which from late 1918 was made a criminal offence under the War Precautions Act, and in the process symbolically recast socialism as a 'foreign' threat. Although critical of the Bolshevik Revolution, the gentle poet, Dick Long, flew the red flag on successive Sundays on the Yarra Bank in defiance of the government proclamation and was imprisoned three times for a total of eight months between December 1918 and December 1919.

The feisty women of the Victorian Socialist Party protested long and loud. A number of them were arrested several times. Among them, Blackburn defended Bella Lavender, teacher and first woman to graduate from an Australian university, and had the charge withdrawn. Another Labor lawyer, Alf Foster defended others. Jennie Baines, who had served time in a London prison as a prominent suffragette, threatened a hunger strike and was fined instead. The printers, Fraser and Jenkinson, were summoned for 'aiding and abetting the flag flying by printing a dodger referring to the Red Flag Day'. Blackburn successfully defended both.[9] Up in Brisbane, where a Labor Government led by T.J. Ryan was in power, several days of rioting followed the gathering at the Trades Hall of a few hundred protesters on 23 March 1919, angry that they could not display the flag.[10] Down in Victoria, though, the more moderate Trades Hall Council chose not to take up the challenge and fly the flag.[11]

Blackburn precisely caught the swirling mix of radicalism and pragmatism in Victoria at this time in his acceptance speech on taking over as ALP president. He was 'pleased' that the annual Party conference had set its feet on 'the right path'. The delegates had chosen to reject capitalism and stand 'frankly for the Co-operative Commonwealth. They had now declared that the Labor Party stands, not to palliate the capitalist system, but to overthrow it'. In this, Blackburn was sending a clear message to the industrial militants agitating for the One Big Union, or fantasising about the immediate ushering in of a Communist utopia. 'The keynote of the Party', he declared, 'must be sane radicalism'.[12]

'Sane radicalism', by which Blackburn meant a strategic pragmatism, was not an easy position to maintain in the immediate post-war years. Long-standing grievances aggravated by sharply rising prices soon 'exploded in the most costly series of strikes Australia had yet known'.[13] Several maritime unions were principal contributors. Seamen felt particularly aggrieved on a number of fronts.[14] They had made an important contribution to the war effort without making any wage claims, but had not benefited from the gratuity awarded to those who had seen active service in uniform. Promised regulations had not been enacted after years of waiting and shipowners were running the seamen to ever-tightening schedules while their profit margins rose rapidly. Spanish flu increased seamen's anxieties. Sailors who fell ill with Spanish Flu were put ashore at the nearest port, without wages, and left to find their own way home.

The intersection of health issues, industrial grievances and increasingly radical unionism dating back to the war years was exemplified by a curtain raiser to the protracted strike in the eastern states. Early in 1919, over in Western Australia, Perth was isolated by efforts to keep the Spanish flu out. The transcontinental railway had been suspended and ships arriving at Fremantle Docks were fumigated and placed in quarantine, leading to food shortages and lack of work for 'lumpers', as the dockworkers were known. When the ship *Dimboola* arrived with urgently needed medical supplies and foodstuffs, an attempt was made to unload them before the quarantine period expired, using non-union labour brought on to the wharves during the 1917 strike. In truth this was more a demarcation dispute than a health issue, but the wharf was picketed by Waterside Workers' Federation (WWF) members, their wives, and a growing band of supporters. Thousands of people took part in demonstrations in late April supporting the 'lumpers', including a march headed by one hundred returned soldiers.

Alerted that police were preparing to clear the wharves, barricades were erected, and violence erupted on Sunday 4 May 1919 when Premier Hal Colebatch arrived in a launch with a party of volunteer labourers in a further attempt to unload the *Dimboola*. They were greeted with a barrage of scrap iron and stone missiles from the bridge above and, in a confrontation known since as 'Bloody Sunday', WWF member Tom Edwards was fatally wounded. A truce was declared, and the non-union labour left the wharves. Indeed most of them left Fremantle in the face of ongoing hostility. 'Bloody Sunday' was considered a victory for the 'lumpers'.[15]

Things were about to get a whole lot worse on the eastern seaboard, where the maritime unions were just as restive and under the influence of radical leaders itching to break out from under what they saw as the straightjacket of the Conciliation and Arbitration Court. In December 1918 the Seamen's Union had submitted a claim to the Court for a fifty per cent wage increase. Mr Justice Higgins handed down an offer of eleven per cent.[16] The federal secretary of the Seamen's Union, militant socialist Tom Walsh, then requested a conference on wages and conditions with the Controller of Shipping, which automatically brought the Commonwealth Government into the negotiations since it had become a large shipowner during the war.

This conference met in April 1919 and the Union demanded a minimum wage of £14 a month for able-bodied seamen, shorter hours, decent living conditions and food, and adequate compensation for illness and death. The union's claims were flatly rejected – most believed on the initiative of the government, because some of the ship owners had already conceded some of these demands – and the men struck in May 1919. *The Age* and Justice Higgins both declared that the main cause of the strike was the 'teachings of overseas theorists',[17] by which they meant British-born activists like Walsh, and some in the Government seemed excessively fearful of their 'Bolshevik' intentions. But it was more the arbitration system than the government itself that Walsh had in his sights, as Justice Higgins certainly understood. 'The Seamen's Union viewed the arbitration system as a straightjacket', *The Socialist* reported 'Instead of pursuing mere crumbs via the bosses' courts, they opted to use their industrial strength'.[18] The goal was direct bargaining, and the strike was a test of strength. Within a few days, men began to walk off the job. Beginning in Queensland the walk-offs soon spread to New South Wales and Victoria.

The effect of the strike, which lasted all winter, was particularly severe in Victoria with its reliance on imported coal to power rail and tramway services and industry. The situation was exacerbated when Victorian wharf labourers went out on strike in support of their fellow unionists in New South Wales where the Government had introduced an anti-union, bureau licensing system on the waterfront. The Victorian Trades Hall Council immediately set up a Wharf Labourers' Relief Committee and before a cheering crowd at a packed rally on 25 May, Blackburn committed the full support of the Victorian Labor Party to the struggle.[19] As with the Seamen, part of the grievance was related to the war, especially the ship owners' policy of preference for returned servicemen over union members.[20] In this case, though, escalation was quickly averted by the appointment in June of a Royal Commission under Mr Justice Dethridge to review stevedoring labour relations in Victoria.[21]

Meanwhile, the consequences of the national Seamen's strike grew steadily more severe for Victorians. By the second week in June 32,500 workers had been stood down including 8,000 women, discharged from clothing factories, and food processing while housewives struggled to keep their families fed and warm.[22] From 3 July power was heavily rationed, even for heating in mid-winter, and demands for relief grew increasingly insistent. Victorian Labor leader Prendergast wondered, with some justification, why brown coal could not be called into service. He saw this failure as a tactic designed to add pressure on the union. Of course, in New South Wales, the interruption of sea trade with Victoria meant that collieries and steelworks remained idle, though the carriage of coal by rail to the Sydney metropolitan area ensured that the effects on industry were less severe than in Victoria. Even so, by 16 June 22 ships were reported strike bound in Sydney.

In South Australia, conditions were less chaotic than in Victoria. Nevertheless by the end of the first week in June an estimated 900 people had been stood down in Adelaide. Supplies of electricity had been reduced by up to 40 per cent and gas by 25 per cent. Cuts in train services meant that for a while railway employees were placed on three-quarter time and those with holiday entitlements were put on immediate leave. In Tasmania, potato cargoes rotted on the wharves, and the Government placed restrictions on the supply of coal.

The effects of the strike were felt more keenly in Western Australia and Northern Queensland, which were entirely dependent on sea transport. News came from Wyndham on the northwest coast was that 400 meat workers were living on meat alone. Diarrhoea was prevalent, and sickness caused a run down in production. The towns of Northern Queensland were similarly affected. On 13 August in the Federal House of Representatives a telegram was read from the Chairman of Hinchinbrooke Shire, Ingham, Queensland:

> No flour procurable here, other foodstuffs almost exhausted, general isolation hospital here full of influenza patients; no butter procurable. Cane cutting proceeding and two mills crushing, storage space scarce, resulting early stoppage of mills; position very serious throughout district.[23]

On 11 August the Queensland Government had proclaimed the requisition of all flour throughout the State.[24] As Blackburn observed, it was 'a melancholy fact that every strike involves in suffering many men and women who have had no voice in its making'.[25]

A generally conciliatory interstate conference of leaders of all the unions whose members were affected by the strike was held on 21 July.[26] It was to no avail since on the following day Tom Walsh, secretary of the Seamen's Union, was jailed for encouraging a strike contrary to the provisions of the Arbitration Act. This was his second challenge to the penal clause. The first time he had only been fined £200 and warned not to do it again. Walsh considered it his duty as a working-class representative who

> understood his position in class society ... to do all I can to bring about the disaster that has been predicted if the lighting supply of the city were cut off. It was the duty of every trade unionist to throw this city into darkness, and to make it impossible for the civil authorities to do without the help and support of the members of the Seamen's Union.[27]

You can see why Walsh was considered dangerous. At one point in this drama, he gave all of the Seamen's Union funds to Blackburn for safekeeping. But Blackburn feared being raided too, so he took the money home and gave it to his wife Doris – who put it in the pram under her younger son Dick.[28]

Walsh pleaded guilty to a second charge and treated the courtroom to a lengthy, impassioned speech.[29] Blackburn, acting as his defence counsel, was requested by the prosecutor, H.E. Starke, to advise his client to adopt a course that would avoid the necessity of a jail sentence. Blackburn replied that it was not for him to tell his client what he should or should not do, but 'personally', if asked to express his opinion, he 'should say he was doing right'.[30] As Blackburn observed later, 'Walsh had deliberately gone to gaol to force the Government's hands'.[31] In any case, he argued, 'It is not by penal clauses that men can be induced to accept arbitration'. Their use only resulted in workers 'becoming saturated with a spirit of mingled distrust for, and contempt of, the law. I speak as one believing', Blackburn went on, 'that an acceptable scheme of arbitration is possible. I believe it is possible to make the inducements to enter the Arbitration Court so great that the unions having freedom to choose between the Court and the strike, will choose the Court'.[32]

Behind the scenes, the Government was more anxious for a settlement than the arrest implied. Or at least some members of it were. In a meeting with Blackburn and the union executive, Acting Prime Minister Senator Edward Millen and the employers conceded almost all the union demands. But the striking seamen refused to return to work while Walsh was in prison. Blackburn visited Walsh and obtained his signature on a statement urging a return to work.[33] 'I am deeply thankful', it read, 'for the staunch friendship of my comrades but trust that they will not let their consideration for me stand in the way of getting justice for themselves and their families. I ask then to leave me and my imprisonment out of the matter'. At the same time a private letter was delivered to the Federal officials by Adela Pankhurst, Walsh's equally, if not more, radical wife, suggesting the opposite.[34] There is no reason to think Blackburn's letter did not contain Walsh's true intent. Federal Labor member, Frank Anstey, himself a former seaman, also sought to intervene.[35] Like Blackburn, Anstey believed Walsh's imprisonment had given the union a tactical advantage that might be lost by rejecting the offer on hand.[36] At meetings in Melbourne in August, addressed by both Anstey and Blackburn, rowdy objections to the involvement of politicians in a purely union matter were raised and a return to work was again rejected.[37] An inconclusive meeting on 17 August agreed to leave the decision to the Sydney seamen.[38]

When Blackburn travelled to Sydney to meet with the strikers he found similar resistance to a return to work, as well as a measure of hostility to his efforts.[39] Nevertheless, after private meetings with the leadership, he returned to Melbourne on 22 August confident that prospects for a resolution were 'most favourable', despite the pessimistic press reports. Blackburn was taken by car from Spencer Street Station to Parliament House[40] to meet with Senator Millen, who gave assurances that unionists would not be directed to man ships on which non-union labour was employed – the final sticking point. Blackburn then telegraphed to the Sydney seamen that he believed Millen was being 'fair and open', and advised a return to work. His advice was accepted – reluctantly.[41] By now it was 26 August. Privately Blackburn had told Millen that if this effort failed, he 'would wash his hands of the whole affair'.[42] On 2 October, Walsh was released from prison as 'an act of leniency'.[43] In the end, in historian Ian Turner's judgment, 'the political honours were about even – the government had preserved the decencies, but everyone knew the seamen had won'.[44]

The Seamen had won on the issue of wages and conditions, and they had certainly secured for themselves a deal outside the compulsory arbitration system, but they were only partially successful in their aim of undermining the power of the Commonwealth Arbitration Court. The intransigence of the ship owners and the government had won widespread support for the Seamen, yet the destructive effects of the strike as it wore on, and the possibility of losing gains made by the labour movement over the previous twenty years, led other unions to work to bring the parties to compromise. Though Blackburn had reservations about the Commonwealth Arbitration system – reservations that prompted him to sketch the basis for a better Arbitration Act in July 1919[45] – at this point, along with Anstey and the leaders of the Victorian Trades Hall Council, he played an important part in moderating the industrial action, without conceding the value of direct negotiation. As he put it later,

> I have sat on strike committees; I have brought strikes to an end, and I have helped to keep strikes going. I helped to bring the seamen's strike of 1919 to an end, and the seamen got what they could not get from the Commonwealth Arbitration Court. They got improved conditions.[46]

One measure of the success of the Seamen's Union challenge was that the Industrial Peace Act, passed in 1920, established special tribunals to deal with intractable disputes. Justice Higgins, who had warned against settlements outside the arbitration system,[47] resigned, protesting that these tribunals would be a 'convenient mode of yielding to strikes without expressly admitting it'.[48]

All this industrial unrest also prompted efforts by the Commonwealth government 'to stabilise the national wage bill by other means'.[49] One such means was a Royal Commission into 'the cost of living in relation to the minimum or basic wage' promised by Prime Minister Hughes during the election campaign of October 1919 and set up under A.B. Piddington, a small 'l' liberal from NSW with a leaning to the left and considerable experience in previous enquiries on employment and arbitration. Unions and employers were each represented by counsel to the Commission. Victorian socialist barrister, Alf Foster, was chosen to act as Union advocate, with Blackburn providing the briefs.[50]

The preparation of briefs for Foster provided Blackburn with substantial additional work in his new legal practice. As part of this work Blackburn engaged closely with the Conference of Federated Unions, most of which, like the Seamen, were unhappy with the operations of the Commonwealth Arbitration Act. For some time he acted as secretary of this body, assisted by a young Albert Monk, who would go on to become a powerful and long-serving president of the ACTU. Blackburn was unhappy that so many 'Arbitrationist Unions' declined to co-operate with the Conference.[51] No doubt he was even more unhappy with 'the miserably weak' resolution passed in December 1920 which called on the Unions to keep the Piddington figures before the Federal and State governments by propaganda, but proposed no stronger action.[52]

The extensive, year-long investigations of the Piddington Commission arrived at the amount of £5 16s a week to keep a man, his wife and three children at an acceptable standard in current prices. It also recommended quarterly adjustments to meet changes in the cost of living.[53] The current basic wage was £3 18s and the NSW Board of Trade had recently announced a finding that £4 5s was a 'living wage'. The Commonwealth Statistician, George Knibbs, reported that the 'whole produced wealth of the country ... would not, if divided equally among employees, yield the necessary amount'.[54] The Prime Minister rejected the sum out of hand, and in the next wage case before him Higgins, who felt the terms of reference of the Piddington Commission had allowed too wide a scope, awarded only £4 4s. The only consolation for workers at this time was the widespread success of campaigns to achieve (briefly) a 44 hour week, or Saturday half holiday.[55] This had been achieved by a mix of direct action and legal argument that would continue to characterise Australian industrial relations.

'Master's Patriotism', a particularly biting cartoon published in the *Australian Seamen's Journal* in 1923, captured the flavour of grievance swirling among unionists in the postwar years. The unions had supported the war effort enthusiastically, and by 1915 over 1,000 seamen had joined the AIF, including John Simpson Kirkpatrick, whose trips with his donkey at Gallipoli had become the stuff of legend.

Blackburn's role in ending the Seamen's Strike was arguably the highpoint of his direct influence in the Labor Party. It also marked a profound deepening of his relationship with the union movement. From this point his closest associates were increasingly drawn from among the leaders and members of trade unions. With their support Blackburn continued to play a leading role in industrial relations as a lawyer and as a member of parliament until his death in 1944.

Notes

1 Ian Turner, *Industrial Labour and Politics: the Dynamics of the Labour Movement in Eastern Australia, 1900–1921* (Sydney: Hale & Iremonger, 1979, 1st edn. 1965), 194–5, 'Table for Strikes 1913–1921', 254.

2 For a detailed analysis of this Strike, especially in Victoria, see Charles Fahey & John Lack, 'The Great Strike of 1917 in Victoria: Looking Fore and Aft, and from Below', *Labour History*, No. 106 (May 2014), 69–97.

3 Civil Rights and Labor History Consortium, University of Washington, 'Seattle General Strike Project', http://depts.washington.edu/labhist/strike/, accessed 16 September 2019.

4 Richard Morris, 'Mr Justice Higgins Scuppered': the 1919 Seamen's Strike', *Labour History*, No. 37, November 1979, 52–62.

5 Brian Fitzpatrick & Rowan Cahill, *The Seamen's Union of Australia, 1872–1972: a history* (Sydney: Seamen's Union of Australia, 1981).

6 For more detailed information on Maurice Blackburn, see http://adb.anu.edu.au/biography/blackburn-maurice-mccrae-5258, and also Carolyn Rasmussen, *The Blackburns: Private Lives, Public Ambition* (Melbourne: MUP, 2019).

7 *Labor Call*, 29 May 1919, 8.

8 *Victorian Parliamentary Debates*, Vol. 177, 17 October 1928, 2332.

9 Bertha Walker, *Solidarity Forever* (Melbourne: National Press, 1972), 124–5.

10 Frank Farrell, *International Socialism & Australian Labour: The Left in Australia* (Sydney: Hale and Iremonger, 1981), 1–2.

11 Paul Strangio, *Neither Power Nor Glory: 100 Years of Political Labor in Victoria, 1856–1956* (Melbourne: MUP, 2012), 129.

12 *Labor Call*, 29 May 1919, 8.

13 Turner, 194.

14 See *Labour Call*, 29 May 1919, 9 for an example of 'The case for the seamen'.

15 David Hutchison, '"Bloody Sunday" revisited', in Paul Arthur Longley & Geoffrey Bolton, *Voices from the West End: Stories, People and Events that Shaped Fremantle* (Perth: WA Museum, 2012), 210–49; David Webb & David Warren 2005, 'The day a wharf dispute erupted into Bloody Sunday', *Fremantle: Beyond the Round House* (Fremantle: Longley), 54–5; David Baker, 'Death by Panic: "Bloody Sunday" on the Fremantle Wharf', in *Police, Picket Lines and Fatalities: Lessons from the Past* (London: Palgrave Pivot, 2014), 36–51. 'The Fremantle Wharf Crisis of 1919'. https://en.wikisource.org/wiki/The_Fremantle_Wharf_Crisis_of_1919, accessed 18 July 2019.

16 Turner, 194–5.

17 *The Age*, 22 May 1919, 6; *Worker*, 5 & 19 June 1919.

18 Anthony Main, 'History: The 1919 seamen's strike', *The Socialist*, 20 May 1919. https://thesocialist.org.au/1919-seamens-strike/.

19 *The Age*, 26 May 1919, 7. See also 'The case for the Wharf Laborers', *Labor Call*, 29 May 1919, 3.

20 *Labor Call*, 29 May 1919, 3.

21 For a full discussion of the issues, see *Report of the Royal Commission in Industrial Troubles on Melbourne Wharfs* (1919, G.J. Dethridge, Commissioner), *Australian Parliamentary Papers*, 1920–21, Vol. IV, 687 ff.

22 *The Age*, 10, 11 June 1919.

23 Morris, 57.

24 Ibid.

25 *Labor Call*, 17 June 1920, 6.

26 *Commonwealth Arbitration Report*, Vol. 13, 1919, quoted in Morris, 57.

27 This is taken from a police report of a series of speeches delivered by Walsh at the Bijou Theatre. Quoted in Morris, 59

28 Rasmussen, 156

29 *The Age*, 23 July 1919, 10.

30 Quoted in Dennis Dodd, '"A Prince for Paupers": A Political Biography of Maurice

Blackburn', PhD, La Trobe University, 1994, 293.

31 *Argus*, 15 August 1919, 7.

32 *Labor Call*, 24 June 1920, 6.

33 *Sydney Morning Herald*, 5 August 1919; *The Age*, 5 August 1919, 5.

34 John Rickard, *H.B. Higgins: The Rebel as Judge* (London: Allen & Unwin, 1984), 251.

35 The offer was communicated to the Government in a 'Secret' ciphered telegram, 8 August 1919, quoted in Dodd, 293.

36 *Argus*, 15 August 1919, 7.

37 See, for example, the report of a meeting on 13 August in the *Argus*, 15 August 1919, 7.

38 *Argus*, 18 August 1919, 7. *The Age*, 18 August, 8 and 19 August 1919, 7.

39 *Argus*, 20 August 1919, 9; *Sydney Morning Herald*, 21 August 1919, 7. See also *Argus*, 25 August 1919 for similar expressions of hostility to Maurice Blackburn.

40 *Argus*, 23 August 1919, 19.

41 *Argus*, 26 August 1919, 4.

42 Quoted in Dodd, 295.

43 *Worker*, 2 October 1919.

44 Turner, 196. See also Morris, 56–62.

45 *Labor Call*, 24 July 1919, 6.

46 *Victorian Parliamentary Debates*, Vol. 179, 30 July 1929, 539.

47 Rickard, 249.

48 From H.B. Higgins, *A New Province for Law and Order* (London: Dawsons of Pall Mall, 1968), 175, quoted in Morris, 61.

49 Ibid.

50 Ibid., 87–94; Graham Morris, *A.B. Piddington: The Last Radical Liberal* (Sydney: UNSW Press, 1995), 79–99.

51 *Labor Call*, 18 March 1920, 11.

52 *Socialist*, 10 December 1920.

53 *Report of Royal Commission on the Basic Wage*, Australian Parliamentary Papers, 1920–1, Vol. IV, 529 ff.

54 Quoted in Constance Lamour, *Labor Judge: The Life and Times of Judge Alfred William Foster* (Sydney: Hale & Iremonger, 1985), 89.

55 Turner, 199–200. Maurice Blackburn provided a history of campaigns for the shorter day over three issues in *Labor Call*, 6 May, 3, 10 June 1920.

Ambit Claims for Reparations

The 'pestiferous varmint' Hughes at Versailles

TONY WARD

> A journey through the devastated areas of France is impressive to the eye and the imagination beyond description. During the winter of 1918–19 … the horror and desolation of war was made visible to sight on an extraordinary scale of blasted grandeur. The completeness of the destruction was evident. For mile after mile nothing was left.[1]

At the end of the First World War, the victorious Allies were determined that Germany should atone for such devastation. So well described by British economist John Maynard Keynes in his 1919 best-seller *The Economic Consequences of the Peace.* But there were considerable debates on the extent of the reparations bill to be handed Germany – and on that country's capacity to pay. The size of reparations became an issue in the later months of 1918, and into the Versailles Peace Conference in 1919. Not least because of a crusade conducted by Australian Prime Minister Billy Hughes, who was in Britain and then France from July 1918 to April 1919.

As is discussed below, Germany ended up paying considerably less than was envisaged at Versailles, or even the lesser sums eventually confirmed two years later. During the 1920s, in slowing, delaying and ultimately evading payment, the German Government made much use of Keynes' *Economic Consequences of the Peace.* The book became a prize exhibit for arguments that the Versailles settlement was unfair. Keynes wrote his polemic from exasperation at what he saw as vengeful claims on Germany at Versailles. Hughes was high on the list of those Keynes blamed for creating these claims.

Focussing on the reparations, this short article argues that Hughes' ambit claim for reparations substantially backfired. Hughes did not create the antagonisms, but he certainly added fuel to the fires. And, rather than winning additional compensation for Australia, the ambit antagonised Keynes amongst others and created a backlash that assisted Germany in paying much less in reparations. This article outlines firstly the background to reparations at Versailles, then at Hughes's efforts. It then looks at Keynes' analysis in *The Economic Consequences of the Peace.* It finally surveys the outcomes in the 1920s.

Background to the reparations

Over the hundred years before the Versailles Conference, Europe had seen many examples of post-war reparations paid by defeated nations. Following Napoleon's defeat at Waterloo, the French had to pay extensive damages and to meet the cost of an occupying army for three years. After its victories in wars in the 1860s, Prussia exacted heavy payments from defeated enemies. As well as being annexed, various previously independent German states had to pay large amounts in indemnities. Following defeat by Prussia in 1870, France not only lost Alsace and Lorraine, but had to pay 20 billion goldmarks, plus costs of occupation.[2] Early in 1918, the German empire imposed major costs on the defeated Soviet Russia. In the Treaty of Brest-Litovsk, Russia ceded 290,000 square miles, one quarter of its population, most of its coal deposits, and all its oil production. After further German advances, in the Treaty of Moscow in August 1918 Russia ceded Georgia and the Crimea, gave Germany exclusive rights to major coal fields, and paid all of its gold and 6 billion marks in reparations.[3]

Compared to this history, the initial claims of the Allies in 1918 were mild indeed. On 8 January 1918, US President Woodrow Wilson announced to Congress his 14 Points to guide post-war settlement. These included:

- In point VII, Belgium to be evacuated by Germany, which would also pay for restoration of war damage.
- In point VIII, all French territory occupied by Germany should be freed, the invaded portions restored, and Alsace-Lorraine returned to France.

At the Armistice, the Allies extended these provisions in conditions handed to a German delegation on 8 November 1918. Wilson's 14 Points were supplemented by the 'Lansing Note'. Referring to points VII and VIII, the note stated:

> The Allied Governments feel that no doubt ought to be allowed to exist as to what this provision implies. By it they understand that compensation will be made by Germany for all damage done to the civilian population of the Allies and their property by the aggression of German by land, by sea, and from the air.[4]

Keynes commented that, at the end of October:

> I do not believe that any responsible statesman had in mind the exaction from Germany of an indemnity for the general costs of the war. They sought only to make it clear (a point of considerable importance to Great Britain) that reparation for damage done to non-combatants and their property was

> not limited to invaded territory ... but applied equally to all such damage, whether 'by land, by sea, or from the air'. It was only at a later stage that a general popular demand for an indemnity, covering the full costs of the war [arose].[5]

That 'general popular demand' had been encouraged by the Australian Prime Minister, Billy Hughes:

> At that juncture there was a clamor from certain quarters that the Government had given by no means sufficiently clear undertakings that they were not going 'to let the Hun off'. Mr Hughes was evoking a good deal of attention by his demands for a very large indemnity, and [newspaper baron] Lord Northcliffe was lending his powerful aid to the same cause.[6]

Hughes had indeed played a significant role.

Hughes in Britain and at Versailles

Hughes addressed Parliament in Melbourne on 10 September 1919. He had been away from Australia for 15 months, since April 1918. In that time, he had visited the US, Britain, and France, and had attended an Imperial Conference in London, and the Versailles Peace Treaty negotiations. Hughes, polishing his image as 'the Little Digger', had a tumultuous welcome home in August 1919. Large crowds applauded his speeches in a progression across the country from Fremantle. All with the spirit described in Melbourne by the *Argus:* 'all the time [the crowd] cheered itself hoarse for the little man'.

In his speech to Parliament, Hughes outlined his three main goals at the end of World War I, which he had pursued at Versailles, and indeed, across the whole trip. The first was for Australia to secure previous German colonies under League of Nations Mandates in Papua New Guinea and other Pacific islands, including Nauru (the latter with valuable phosphate resources). The second was to protect the White Australia policy, especially from a Japanese proposal that racial equality be included in the Preamble to the new League of Nations covenant. The third goal was to seek reparations from Germany for the costs of the war.

Hughes was broadly successful in the first two, but, despite the cheering crowds, was much less so in the third. As Carl Bridge has argued, Hughes' successes came where his interests aligned with others' agendas:

> His success over the Pacific Islands Mandate owed much to the backing of the British Empire, France, Italy and Japan. He needed Dominion and United States backing to defeat the racial equality clause and guarantee White Australia. Without British and American backing he failed dismally over reparations.[7]

In pursuing his goals, Hughes employed the temperament and oratory skills that had led the *Sydney Morning Herald* in 1910 to describe him as a 'fiery particle'[8], and David Low in 1916 to draw a famous cartoon of British Empire leaders at the Imperial Conference cowering before a Hughes tirade. In early 1919 at Versailles, Hughes and Woodrow Wilson had heated exchanges over the Mandate question. Wilson privately termed him a 'pestiferous varmint'.[9]

Hughes' fiery speeches in England in 1916 had attracted comment beyond Low's cartoon, and some downside. In October 1916, a mutual repatriation scheme enabled some British and Australian civilians, marooned in Germany since the start of the war, to return to Britain. On her return, one reported that 'Mr Hughes, the Australian Minister, is hated in Germany, and matters became worse for Australian prisoners after his speeches in London'. Such was the mood of the time in Melbourne, that the *Argus* newspaper reported the story with a headline 'Hun compliment to Mr Hughes'.[10]

In the latter part of 1918, Hughes spoke a number of times around Britain, demanding tough measures against all German interests. He 'advocated a strong line with Germany over trade, colonies and reparations. Had not the Germans themselves imposed a Carthaginian Treaty on the Russians at Brest-Litovsk?'[11] In October, Hughes met with the French cabinet and encouraged them to make harsh demands on Germany. Even for war-time jingoism, some of the vitriol went too far. One company had previously been part of a German combine but had reorganised itself on British lines at the start of the war, under the name Merton and company. Hughes publicly criticised Merton for alleged German ties. Merton sued for libel, with a post-war settlement that cost the Australian government £6,500.[12]

But Hughes' rhetoric had a marked effect on the political environment in Britain during the November-December 1918 'khaki' election. Before the campaign, at the Armistice, Prime Minister Lloyd George supported reparations only to cover the costs of direct material damage.[13] From 7 November, Hughes made several speeches publicly demanding Germany pay the costs of the war. Lloyd George appointed Hughes chair of a committee to assess war damages. The hard-line committee reported in early December, assessing the damages at £24 billion (then equivalent to $125 billion), and arguing Germany should be made to pay £1.2 billion annually, a sum the British War Cabinet described as 'wild and fantastic'.[14] Nonetheless, Lloyd George toughened his stance during the campaign. By the end of November, he could have been echoing Hughes' arguments that Germany should pay the full costs of the Allied war efforts. On 11 December, he was promising to 'search German pockets'.[15] Bellicose demands urged 'hang the Kaiser' and 'make Germany pay fully for the costs of the war'.[16] A senior Minister proclaimed 'We will get out of her all you can squeeze out of a lemon and a bit more … I will squeeze her until you can hear the pips squeak'.[17]

Following a landslide electoral victory on 14 December 1918, Lloyd George faced the need to deal with the demons he, with Hughes and others, had unleashed. The main stage now moved to Versailles and the

Peace Conference. There, on 10 February 1919, Hughes became chair of a committee assessing reparations, with some fellow hardliners as members. The committee initially discussed estimates as high as $120 billion, with 'Hughes proudly demanding more money from the Germans than anyone else'.[18] The sums included some disingenuous figures. For but one example, John Maynard Keynes noted that Belgium had not suffered complete devastation, unlike north eastern France. Nonetheless, some 'Belgian claims against Germany amounting to a sum in excess of the total estimated pre-war wealth of the whole country'.[19] Such 'simply irresponsible' claims were later reduced to a total reparations bill of $47 billion – and even that attracted the ire of Keynes.[20]

Keynes and the economic consequences of Versailles

Keynes was a leading UK Treasury official at the Versailles negotiations. Critical of both the proceedings and results, he later wrote the scathing *The Economic Consequences of the Peace.* Published in December 1919, it became an unlikely best seller, and, in the words of Keynes' biographer, 'one of the most influential books of the twentieth century'. By August 1920, it had been translated into 12 languages, including German, and sold a total of well over 100,000 copies.[21]

Keynes saw a stark contrast between two possible approaches to a Peace Treaty. The first, which he supported, stressed the need to establish a prosperous post war Europe. This included a level of German reparations, which Keynes estimated, from both physical damage levels and on capacity to pay, at some $10 billion. But the emphasis was on getting the European economy moving again. In Chapter 7 'Remedies' of his *Economic Consequences of the Peace,* Keynes argued for improved European cooperation on coal and iron; a free trade area encompassing much of Europe; a writing down of inter-Allied war debts; and a new international loan to assist war-ravaged areas to recover.[22]

Such a program has some marked similarities to policies in western Europe after the Second World War. But in both 1919 and 1945, the program required substantial US financial compromises. In 1945, that was forthcoming due in no little part to the strong military threat of the Soviet Union and the political strength of Communist parties in France, Italy and Greece.[23] In the absence of those threats in 1919, the US was in no mood to compromise on debts owed by France and the UK. Nor was the US prepared to countenance a Keynes plan to let Britain and France swap reparations owed by Germany to them for the debts they owed the United States.[24] Over the following few years, there was to be a strong 'connection between French "intransigence" on the reparation issue and American "obstinacy" concerning payment of inter-Allied debts'.[25]

The alternative was often referred to as a Carthaginian Peace, referring to the total destruction of Carthage by Rome after the Third Punic War in 146 BC. Keynes contended that the three key leaders at Versailles were faced with 'An inefficient, unemployed, disorganized Europe … torn by internal strife and international hate, fighting, starving, pillaging, and lying'.[26] But they were little concerned with the future of Europe. Rather, they:

> paid no attention to these issues, being preoccupied with others – Clemenceau to crush the economic life of his enemy, Lloyd George to do a deal and bring home something which would pass muster for a week, the President to do nothing that was not just and right. It is an extraordinary fact that the fundamental economic problems of a Europe starving and disintegrating before their eyes, was the one question [which they ignored].[27]

On reparations, Hughes and his committee found quick support from the French:

> The lead was taken by the French, in the sense that it was generally they who made in the first instance the most definite and the most extreme proposals. This was partly a matter of tactics. When the final result is expected to be a compromise, it is often prudent to start from an extreme position; and the French anticipated at the outset – like most other persons – a double process of compromise, first of all to suit the ideas of their allies and associates, and secondly in the course of the Peace Conference proper with the Germans themselves.[28]

But the French, as with Hughes, were to find their ambit claims too ambitious. Keynes argued the amounts were well beyond any capacity of Germany to pay.

Keynes' analysis of the economic capacity of Europe, and particularly Germany, has been criticised as being too pessimistic. In 1945, French economist Etienne Mantoux wrote *The Carthaginian Peace, or the Economic Consequences of Mr Keynes.* In it he noted the post-war recovery of the German economy. By the late 1920s, both iron and steel production were above 1914 levels, and the German merchant shipping fleet had almost regained its pre-war size.[29] From such details, other writers have argued that Germany could well have afforded a modest increase in taxation to meet reparation demands.[30] And if later historians have qualified his analysis, at the time Keynes' book was certainly influential. Beyond its impressive sales, it 'shaped the policy debates of the 1920s and 1930s, both encapsulating and fostering the mentality favouring appeasement of Germany, a frame of mind that dominated Britain's foreign policy between the wars'.[31] Further, in two key regards, Keynes' analysis was correct. The Reparation Commission agreed with his assessment that the reparation levels talked of at Versailles were well above what Germany could afford. And secondly, the apparently vengeful Treaty did indeed engender considerable antagonism. Adam Tooze argues that 'no single individual did more to undermine the political legitimacy of the Versailles peace than Keynes'.[32]

There is wisdom too in his view of a dark future:

> If we aim deliberately at the impoverishment of Central Europe, vengeance, I dare predict, will not limp. Nothing can then delay for very long that final civil war between the forces of Reaction and the despairing convulsions of Revolution, before which the horrors of the late German war will fade into nothing, and which will destroy, whoever is victor, the civilization and the progress of our generation.[33]

Reparations: the outcomes

The extent of the final reparations amounts was much less than Keynes had feared and criticised. Despite this, successive German governments portrayed them as onerous, and did what they could to delay payments, including using Keynes' book as part of their PR efforts.

The Peace Treaty did not specify an amount for Germany to pay, beyond an interim down payment of 20 billion goldmarks. Article 231 asserted the principle of the 'responsibility of Germany and her allies for causing all the loss and damage to which the Allied and Associated Governments and their nationals have been subjected'. However, Article 232 accepted there were substantial limits on war-weary Germany's capacity to meet onerous reparations. In consequence, Article 233 established a Reparations Commission, to assess both claims and Germany's capacity to pay, and to decide on final payment amounts by May 1921. The Reparations Commission announced in April 1921 the reparations liabilities. However, as Sally Marks' comprehensive analysis of the reparation payments shows, considerable subterfuge was involved.[34]

The headline figure that Germany owed was set at 132 billion gold marks (some $33 billion). As Keynes suggested in a follow up book *A Revision of the Treaty*, this reflected a political judgement of the lowest amount public opinion, especially in France and Belgium, would tolerate[35]. But this total was a chimera. The Commission considered that Germany's capacity to pay was 50 billion goldmarks (some $12.5 billion – only slightly above Keynes' suggestion of $10 billion), similar to what Germany had itself offered in negotiations. The 50 billion figure was established as active A and B bonds, on which payments were scheduled. The remaining 82 billion was designated as C bonds, with no payment schedule established.[36] From the start, actual payments were well below the agreed amounts. By April 1921, Germany had paid only 8 billion of the 20 billion goldmarks the Versailles Treaty had specified as an immediate payment. By the beginning of 1923, the Reparations Commission found Germany in default on agreed supplies of timber and coal (which were used as payments in kind).[37] On 11 January 1923, French, Belgian, and Italian troops and engineers occupied the Ruhr to obtain the coal.

The Reich Chancellery archives indicate that in 1922 and 1923 German leaders chose to postpone tax reform and currency stabilization measures in hopes of obtaining substantial reductions in reparations.[38] The key question was not the capacity to pay, but the willingness to pay. And in the early 1920s, the Weimar government resisted budget and currency reform 'mainly because that way it could escape reparations'.[39] These efforts mirrored a publicity campaign attacking the Versailles Treaty. In that, the Germans made use of Keynes' book.[40] Historian Antony Lentin pondered in 2012: 'It would be a melancholy pastime to speculate … on the value to the Wehrmacht of *The Economic Consequences of the Peace*'.[41]

Following the hyperinflation in Germany in 1923, a new schedule of payments was developed as the Dawes Plan, under US patronage. The Plan, unveiled in April 1924, established stricter oversight of German finances, and a new payment schedule. Germany would pay one billion marks the first year, chiefly out of a new international loan, increasing amounts for the next three years, and then annual payments of 2.5 billion goldmarks, to be increased if the German economy prospered. Once that was reached, the occupation of the Ruhr would end.[42] Another revision occurred in early 1929, following further German complaints about its capacity to pay. The Young Plan set new levels of annuities, all below the Dawes 2.5 billion. However only about one-third of each annuity was unconditionally payable, the remainder could be postponed under conditions of economic or monetary distress. Effectively, under the Young plan, Germany was paying less than half what she would have owed under the Dawes Plan.[43] The turmoil of the Great Depression interrupted these payments. US President Herbert Clark Hoover proposed a moratorium on payments from July 1931. A year later, the Lausanne Conference in June 1932 proposed a 'lasting settlement', whereby Germany was to make a final lump sum payment of three billion gold marks once the convention was ratified. But it was never ratified, and Germany never paid the three billion.[44] In total, Germany paid a little over 20 billion gold marks or $5 billion. This was predominantly financed by foreign loans, many of which were eventually unilaterally cancelled by Hitler.[45]

Early in the 1920s, the German government, rather than strive for sound public finances, sought to demonstrate that it was broke. For instance, Karl Joseph Wirth, chancellor in 1921–22, argued against raising revenues through a property tax, which would have helped slow the collapse of the mark: 'The goal of our entire policy must be the dismantling of the London ultimatum', he declared, and he thought it would be a mistake to suggest, by stabilising the currency, that payments were '80 per cent possible'.[46] Jurgen Tampke describes 'a long and skilfully conducted public relations exercise by the Germans to discredit the Versailles Treaty'.[47]

Conclusion

In 1936, storm clouds were gathering again over Europe. Elizabeth Wiskemann, a correspondent for *The Economist*, met Keynes in London. Referring to *The Economic Consequences* and the ways German politicians had used it, she said: 'I do wish you had not written that book'. In her memoirs, Wiskemann said she 'then longed for the ground to swallow me up'. But Keynes replied, 'simply and gently', 'So do I'.[48] Keynes, in his *General Theory of Employment, Interest and Money* (also from 1936) paid tribute to the power of ideas: 'Madmen in authority, who hear voices in the air, are distilling their frenzy from some academic scribbler of a few years back'.[49] Nevertheless, *The Economic Consequences* fed into, and reinforced, grievances that were already there.

And if we can't be fully sure of what Europe would have looked like without Keynes' book, we similarly can't be sure of the impact of Hughes' vituperative oratory before, and doggedness at, Versailles. Hughes too built on existing grievances – but also reinforced them, given them extra life. And it was the strength of those grievances that pushed Keynes into writing his book. Ambit claims are frequently part of negotiating tactics. But they should be aware of context – pushed too far, they can encourage even greater and opposite reactions. Hughes at Versailles had successes, but on the issue of reparations, his enthusiastic interventions ended up encouraging results that were the opposite of what he wanted. Hughes ended up fouling his own nest.

Notes

1 John Maynard Keynes, *The Economic Consequences of the Peace* (London: Macmillan, 1919), 58.

2 Jurgen Tampke, *A Perfidious Distortion of History: The Versailles Peace Treaty and the Success of the Nazis* (Melbourne: Scribe, 2017), 121–3.

3 Ibid., 82–3.

4 Ibid., 88. The name of the note came from US Secretary of State Robert Lansing, who drafted it.

5 Keynes, *The Economic Consequences of the Peace*, 55, and similarly 65.

6 Ibid., 66.

7 Carl Bridge, *William Hughes: Australia* is one of a series of books on the peace conferences of 1919–23 and their aftermath (London: Haus, 2011), 102–3. The alliance between Wilson and Hughes on the race question is also discussed in e.g. Adam Tooze, *The Deluge: The Great War, America and the remaking of the Global Order 1916–31* (New York: Penguin, 2014), 325.

8 Cited in Bridge, *William Hughes*, 24.

9 Tampke, *A Perfidious Distortion*, 109.

10 *Argus*, 18 October 1916, 9.

11 Bridge, *William Hughes*, 57.

12 Ibid., 61.

13 Keynes, *The Economic Consequences of the Peace*, 65.

14 Robert Skidelsky, *Keynes: Hopes Betrayed 1883–1920* (London: Macmillan, 1992), 356.

15 Tooze, *The Deluge*, 249.

16 Tampke, *A Perfidious Distortion*, 102.

17 Keynes, *The Economic Consequences of the Peace*, 67–8, and Skidelsky *Keynes: Hopes Betrayed*, 356.

18 Phillip A. Dehne, *After the Great War: Economic Warfare and the Promise of Peace in Paris 1919* (London: Bloomsbury, 2019), ch. 2 'Getting Down to Business: January', sections 'Dealing with the Difficult Dominions'. As this book was not available in hardcover or pdf at the time of writing, the Kindle version is referenced.

19 Keynes, *The Economic Consequences of the Peace*, 59.

20 Tampke, *A Perfidious Distortion*, 125–6.

21 Skidelsky, *Keynes: Hopes Betrayed*, 384, 394. Tooze, *The Deluge*, 295 describes sales as 'in the hundreds of thousands'. As Skidelsky had access to Keynes' papers, his estimate is preferred.

22 Keynes, *The Economic Consequences of the Peace*, ch. 7, 121ff, and Skidelsky, *Keynes: Hopes Betrayed*, 316.

23 See for example, Tooze, *The Deluge*, 281, 291.

24 Skidelsky, *Keynes: Hopes Betrayed*, 369. See also the discussion in Tooze, *The Deluge*, 297, 303, 366.

25 Dan P. Silverman, *Reconstructing Europe after the Great War* (Boston: Harvard, 1982), 198.

26 Keynes, *The Economic Consequences of the Peace*, 118.

27 Ibid., 108.

28 Ibid., 14.

29 'Versailles revisited: What if the Allies had been more generous in 1919?' *The Economist*, 6 July 2019, and see detailed discussion in Tampke, e.g. 152, 207–10.

30 Tampke, *A Perfidious Distortion*, 210.

31 Dehne, *After the Great War*, Introduction, 2.

32 Tooze, *The Deluge*, 295.

33 Keynes, *The Economic Consequences of the Peace*, 128.

34 Sally Marks, 'The Myths of Reparations', *Central European History*, Vol. 11, No. 3, 1998, 231–55.

35 John Maynard Keynes, *A Revision of the Treaty* (London: Macmillan, 1922), 39, cited by Marks 236, and see also Robert Skidelsky, *Keynes: the Economist as Saviour 1920–1937* (London: Macmillan, 1992), 54–5.

36 Marks, 'The Myths of Reparations', 237.

37 Ibid., 240.

38 Ibid., 239.

39 Tampke, *A Perfidious Distortion*, 171. In fact, both Britain and France were at the

same time also using delaying tactics over debts to the United States: see Silverman *Reconstructing Europe*, 146.

40 Tooze, *The Deluge,* 295–6.

41 Anthony Lentin, 'Treaty of Versailles: Was Germany Guilty?', *History Today*, Vol. 62, Issue 1, January 2012.

42 Marks, 'The Myths of Reparations', 248.

43 Ibid., 250–1.

44 Ibid., 253.

45 Ibid., 254.

46 'Versailles revisited', *The Economist,* 6 July 2019.

47 Tampke, *A Perfidious Distortion*, 101.

48 Wiskemann, *The Europe I Saw*, 53, cited in Tampke, *A Perfidious Distortion*, 297 footnote 31.

49 John Maynard Keynes, *The General Theory of Employment, Interest and Money* (London: Palgrave, 1936).

1919 – Empires, Revolutions, and the Origins of Fascism

Upheaval and reaction in East Asia, America, and Europe

DAVID PALMER

The year 1919 was the epicentre of a pivotal era in the twentieth century, a turning point when upheavals shook the world.[1] In the wake of the Great War's end, the shock of the Bolshevik Revolution, and the re-division of the globe through the Treaty of Versailles, old empires disappeared (the Austro-Hungarian, Russian, Hapsburg, and Ottoman Empires); new powerful empires emerged (Imperial Japan and the United States); and the existing British and French empires encountered new competition for global colonial control. This shift in power among empires led to new popular resistance that fuelled nationalist independence movements in colonies and imperialist spheres of control beyond Europe and America; revolution and reaction in Central and Southern Europe; and unprecedented class and racial conflict that was met by reaction in the United States. The evolution of far right movements into Axis-era fascism has been well documented, but how big business related to this trend needs greater attention from historians, although some new significant studies have been undertaken.[2]

My focus here is on developments in countries of three regions where significant parallels of 'upheaval and reaction' during 1919: in East Asia – China, Korea, Japan; in North America – the United States; and in Europe – Germany, Italy, and Hungary. What follows is an outline of what I anticipate in future will be an extended and detailed comparative analysis.

Europe, America, East Asia – three regions and examples of seven countries

Europe experienced short-lived revolutions in Germany (the Spartikus Uprising in Berlin led by Communists Luxemburg and Liebknecht, and later brief Communist uprisings in other regions), Italy (the factory councils led by Socialists including Gramsci), and Hungary (Bela Kuhn's Soviet Republic). These were destroyed and led to counter-revolutions that created unstable governments and eventually fascism, first in Italy and subsequently in Germany and Hungary. Both Hitler and Mussolini made their political appearance in this year, with Mussolini's Fascist groups attacking Socialists in Milan and Turin – and Mussolini founding the *Fasci di Combattimento* in March in Milan, while Hitler rose to prominence in the Munich chaos and repression that defeated a far left local government perceived as connected to the Berlin Communists. Other Central and Eastern European countries – Austria and Romania in particular – followed Hungary's shift to the far right in the following decades, opening the way for the Third Reich's expansion through cooperation of pro-fascist regimes that paved the way for invasions.[3]

In the United States a massive strike wave led by progressive American Federation of Labor (AFL) craft unions, Socialists and I.W.W. syndicalists in industries crucial for war production ended in repression and conservative rule but laid the foundations for the rise of industrial unionism a decade later during President Franklin D. Roosevelt's sweeping New Deal reforms. Race riots and extensive attacks on Black communities in 1919 defined repression in the U.S. as well, but laid the groundwork for the later civil rights movement that extended from the Great Depression through the 1950s and 1960s. In contrast to earlier white riots attacking African Americans, the 1919 white rioters in places like Chicago encountered black veterans who had fought in Europe and were armed, and knew how to shoot those invading their neighbourhoods. Both the trade union and civil rights movements came to define American liberal democracy by the late twentieth century, however fragile that democracy became by the twenty first century. The 'Red Scare' arrests and deportations of left-wing socialists and anarchists of 1919 presaged the 1950s anti-communist McCarthy era, but resistance to this type of repression also prepared the ground for the leading role of the Communist Party USA in labour struggles of the Great Depression and later in the 1960s and 1970s for New Left activists in antiwar, community and labour activity – these later left wing groups, in separate eras, openly supporting 'revolution' in word, if not deed.[4]

In East Asia, the nationalist independence movements in China (the May Movement) and Korea (the March First Movement) against Imperial Japan's colonial control and domination created conditions for the rise of revolutionary movements but also reaction in Japan that paved the way for Imperial Fascism by the late 1930s.[5] China's 'Cultural Renaissance' of 1919 became the inspiration for the movement that brought forth intellectuals like Lu Hsun, revered as modern China's greatest pre-World War II writer.[6] This national movement eventually united workers, peasants, intellectuals, and pro-Chinese business people in the resistance to Japan during the Second Sino-Japanese War. These developments were followed by the defeat of pro-US Nationalist forces after World War II, and then the 1949 victory of the Communist revolution and China's rise as a fully independent country.

The case of Korea is particularly important, as it was the Korean March First Movement against Japan that inspired the Chinese May Fourth Movement to boycott Japanese goods.[7] Mao Tse-tung later described the May Fourth Movement as 'a new stage in China's bourgeois-democratic revolution against imperialism and feudalism.'[8] Both movements had a popular base and were directed against Japan – for Koreans against

Japanese colonialism, for Chinese against Japanese economic dominance in port concessions. Both movements were dominated by students and intellectuals, many of whom would later join revolutionary movements in which peasant and worker numbers were far greater. Korea's March First Movement began as a boycott but turned into an independence movement. Two decades earlier, in 1894, following Japan's defeat of China in the First Sino-Japanese War, Japan had imposed hegemony over Korea. By 1905 Japan had made Korea a protectorate under the empire, and in 1910 Japan annexed Korea, making it a colony but claiming that it was an extension of Imperial Japan.[9] As a consequence, all the Great Powers refused to accept Korea as an independent nation, and Korean delegates were refused an audience at Versailles.[10] Korea's resistance to Japanese colonialism as *national* identity was born in 1919 with the March First Movement. In response, Japanese authorities brutally suppressed political protests, and imposed total social and culture control over Koreans, by the 1930s even prohibiting the teaching of Korean as Japanese was the required language in schools.

Japan's accelerated drive for empire on the Asian mainland after World War I was in part a consequence of the Entente powers' refusal to accept Japan's clause against racial discrimination during the Versailles Treaty negotiations. The refusal was led by Britain in response to complaints from Australia's Prime Minister Billy Hughes who told Lloyd George that this would erode the White Australia Policy that excluded Asian immigration. Japan's defeat in the Pacific War in 1945 led to independence for Korea and an end to the Japanese Empire. But Korea was divided into two occupation zones under the rival Cold War superpowers, the US and Soviet Union, which led to the Korean War in 1949. Still unresolved, this division between Communist North and pro-American South has at times been overridden by a common nationalist sentiment born in 1919 against Japanese colonialism, and a nationalist sentiment spanning South and North that continues to be a major factor in normalization efforts and the aspiration for unification of the peninsula.

The managerial revolution and the reshaping of big business in three regions

'Empire' by 1919 no longer was confined to direct administrative control of colonies and colonialism alone, even though every empire in that year had colonies. The political economy underlying control of these colonies and colonized parts of countries, which came to be understood as 'imperialism' during the 1900s and was a term embraced by elites at that time, was grounded in the capitalist economies of the major powers. The major institutions of this new type of capitalism were governments (with their military and diplomats – 'guns' and 'treaties' as enforcers) and big business. Behind every upheaval, whether in Europe, the U.S., or East Asia, were the interests of big business expansion advantaged by government use of force.

Germany's giant businesses survived the Great War, and by the mid-1920s had changed into their modern form. The most significant example was the survival of I.G. in 1919, which was still dominated by individual owners, into a managerially sophisticated business renamed I.G. Farben in 1925, the country's most powerful business giant and a global leader in chemicals and later to play a major role in the Nazi economy.

From 1900 to 1917 America's corporations underwent a 'managerial revolution' that Alfred D. Chandler has described as multiunit business enterprises, creation of managerial hierarchies directed by salaried managers with technical expertise, and the separation of ownership and management. The example of J.P. Morgan illustrates this remarkable transformation of big business. Morgan's bank was the main financer of Entente debt during the Great War before U.S. government lending replaced wartime financial aid to Britain and France. His business empire included U.S. Steel, the world's largest corporation in 1900, but by the 1920s it faced competition from Bethlehem Steel, a company that had adopted a far more efficient management structure. Both U.S. Steel and Bethlehem were strong opponents of unions that led the national steel strike in 1919. Both companies relied on raw materials that included mines in Latin America, a part of the globe where the United States had unrivalled hegemony politically and economically.

In Japan the Mitsubishi and Mitsui *zaibatsu* (with their internal banks, vast industrial operations, and extensive shipping capabilities) benefited from Japanese control of Korea and penetration of Manchuria and Chinese port regions, whether for iron ore and coal, agricultural and industrial production, or shipping access. Both of these *zaibatsu* were the main influences in late Meiji, Taisho, and early Showa government cabinets and in the two rival parties in the Diet.[11]

Every major upheaval of 1919 in the regions and countries used as examples in this analysis threatened these giant corporations' control of resources, labour, and political backing. These businesses, with their new structures, managerial methods, and advanced technology, required political links to operate, whether in dealing with unions organizing in their national plants and facilities, or overseas where they acquired raw materials. The political reaction to resistance against the economic power of big business encouraged the rise of far right and racial nationalism, trends that fuelled movements that eventually led to fascism. While big businesses were not the cause of fascism or fascist movements, over time big business found common ground against a perceived mutual enemy – whether labour movements, left-wing political movements, or revolutionary nationalist movements. The turning point for this development was in 1919, or to be more precise what can be considered the 'era of 1919' encompassing 1914 to the early 1920s when resistance became global, however diverse regionally. But the year 1919 marked the major shift within that era, which can be considered the key moment of change into the twentieth century, including the moment of the origin of fascism.

'There was no "Fascism" anywhere in Europe before the end of the First World War,' according to historian F.L. Carsten, writing in 1971. 'Without the slightest doubt, it was this great upheaval, the destruction and the crises resulting from it, and the fear of "red" revolution which arose in many European countries, that brought forth the movement which – after the Italian example – we call "Fascist".'[12] My contention is that this 'fear' was *global* and was not confined to Europe. In part the threat was aimed at established and new empires – the new anti-colonial nationalist movements, and in part the threat was seen as coming out of the 1917 Bolshevik Revolution in Russia that by 1919 had become an international war of intervention by all the Great Powers seeking its defeat. Even though Britain finally withdrew troops and aid to the White Russian anti-Bolshevik forces that year, Japan had sent 72,000 troops into Siberia.[13] But beyond the immediate fear of the Bolshevik Revolution and the rise of global communism, identifying the origins of fascism and the relationship of big business to the rise of fascist political movements has been highly contested terrain for scholars.[14]

Corporations and national varieties of capitalism and of fascism. Are there linkages?

Business historian Alfred D. Chandler Jr has characterized distinct global characteristics of the managerial revolution. He identified the United States as *competitive capitalism*: huge industrial and financial institutions organized along particular sectors but which must adhere to anti-trust laws, even though these were regularly evaded. This change in the newly emerging modern corporation was consolidated by 1917. For Germany he used the description *cooperative capitalism*, where industrial giants worked in a kind of 'community of interests', or *Interessengemeinschaften*. This trend was consolidated by 1924 following the end of economic chaos resulting from punitive measures of the Versailles Treaty aimed at Germany.[15] For Japan, the huge *zaibatsu* trusts, particularly Mitsubishi, Mitsui, and Sumitomo, stretched across all industrial, commercial, and financial sectors, with internal banks to finance their operations. By the 1920s, companies within each major *zaibatsu* were run by professional managers even as family heads still made key decisions at the top in cooperation with top managers. My own view of the Japanese variant is that it was *financial clan capitalism* (*zaibatsu* literally means 'financial clan / clique').

This was cooperative capitalism *within* the *zaibatsu*, but competitive *among rival zaibatsu*. Japan and its main *zaibatsu* gained from war production needs of the Great War, and gained further from Japan's consolidation of its control of its colonies of Korea and Taiwan, and its new penetration into Manchuria and China. While families controlled at the top, the re-made *zaibatsu* of the 1920s employed professional managers with engineering and financial experience at upper levels to run the companies under the *zaibatsu* trust umbrella.

Numerous scholars have identified types of fascism, but they have generally confined their examples to Europe in the interwar and World War II eras. I advocate a broader global definition, and one that is not confined to these eras though originating in the aftermath of World War I. Fascism can be understood as a particular political framework that has capitalism – and private big businesses – as its economic foundation, though the state determines the economic agenda of production and shapes the labour system, combining waged, forced, and slave labour during wartime.[16] The absence of free, independent trade unions and high levels of union membership are crucial to the establishment of the political economy of fascism, which then facilitates total control at the political level. This demands the elimination of basic legal and human rights, a police state to maintain this regime, and an ideology that is designed for patriotism based on racial nationalism. For major empires that are fascist the factor of empire, and war for empire, is a way to maintain the power of the regime, although overextension has historically been the Achilles heal of all empires, not just fascist ones of the past, a history that spans Rome through the United States today.

The failure of fascist movements in United States to gain total political power (except in the racially segregated South),[17] in contrast to their success in gaining power in Europe and Japan, cannot be separated from these countries' empires and their expansion through force and economic coercion. Levels of internal citizen movements and dissent, along with viable political opposition and legal constraints, have acted as a check on empire, as the history of both the U.S. and Britain indicate. Their absence is a hallmark of traditional fascist empires. In this sense, the political movements and legal histories of countries have had their own trajectories. But fascists movements also have been shaped by the history of state interactions and the perceived success or failure of 'empire' and praise or blame related to these dynamics: German defeat attributed to traitors and the oppression of Versailles Treaty reparations followed by French troops occupying the Ruhr; or Japan's alliance that assisted the Entente but was followed by constraints on the expansion of its empire into China and Manchuria imposed by Versailles, while refusing inclusion in the Treaty of a non-discrimination clause to end Asian exclusion by the West. Nor can the revolutions in each region (for workers' political power in Central Europe; for workplace democracy and against racial oppression in the U.S.; for national independence in Korea and China), some of them virtual civil wars, others militant mass protests – be separated from the role of empire.

In *each country* most progressive movements were initially defeated, but the extent of the defeat is an open question. These movements had vast differences within them, some advocating moderate reforms (American workers), others wanting worker control of production short of revolution (Italy), and still others advocating the radical overthrow of the state (Germany). In Asia these movements were multi-class and encompassed both urban and rural populations, with a focus as much on national independence as economic needs. Each region and country had different cultures, distinct forms of government and law, but the *common* factor in each, whether industrialized (U.S., Western Europe, Japan) or colony / semi-colony (China, Korea, and most of the rest of Asia), was the existence of big business as the core element of the political economy of empire. The *difference* was whether progressive movements in the long run could prevail (as in the United States during the Great Depression and under New Deal policies, China in 1945 and again in 1949, Korea by 1945 only with Japanese surrender) or suffered total defeat (Italy by 1924, Germany by 1933, Japan by the late 1930s, Korea during the Korean War, and then in the South until the democratic popular uprisings of the late 1980s). The absence of democracy in communist China and North Korea, beyond the scope of this paper, deserves discussion in another context.

Political economy and the role of big business – a key to the problem?

The unanswered question is how this common factor – big business – could be so consistent *internationally* in the era of 1919 (1914 to the early 1920s) in terms of management, production, technology such as in steel, shipbuilding, electrical machinery, and chemicals – in contrast to radically different government regimes relying on these big businesses after 1919. This divergence (big industrial business international convergence versus political regimes) accelerated during the 1920s and culminated in the late 1930s and the era of World War II.

One might argue that 'business' operated in a different realm to government – one focused on production and the market, the other on gaining power and seeking popular support. But big business interests were prominent in every country considered here as case studies. The full answer requires further detailed study of the relationship between business elites and political leaders (in government or in emerging movements). This has been done to some extent for Germany, but not for Japan. For the United States the question is more problematic as there has never been a total fascist government in power. An exception was the American South, where African Americans in the segregationist era were subjected to terrorist violence (KKK and white vigilantes) backed by local and state authorities, deprived of the franchise, subjected economically, and by law were racially segregated from all public facilities. But the American South was outside the core power nexus of big business in strategic industries in the era of the Great War and 1920s, even though plants and facilities of major corporations were located in the region.[18]

What might be the relevance of 1919 for our world today?

Understanding the developments of 'upheaval and reaction' in these regions and countries within them challenges the view that 'revolution' and 'fascism' should not only be viewed as historically and geographically specific to Europe. 'Fascism' was not solely European while Japan was not just 'militarist.' By contrast, 'revolution' has been universally recognised as an international phenomenon not restricted to a particular era or part of the globe. But fascism was a system, some would argue, while revolution is an event. To the contrary, fascism has been an event and a movement that evolved into a system, while revolution has generally been organised with effective institutions to finally succeed. Revolutions without military power and political organisation rarely succeed, although one could say that current revolutions at least require military neutrality (as in the case of the transition away from fascism in Spain and Chile in the second half of the twentieth century).

It is a mistake to view fascism as confined solely to a previous era far distant from our own. A few decades ago the terms 'capitalism' and 'working class' were seen as ideological and to be avoided by those with mainstream views, instead using the euphemisms 'free markets' and 'middle class.' But in our own time these terms once deemed 'communist' are commonly used by economists such as Thomas Piketty and politicians of the right, centre and left in every country including the United States. Since the U.S. election of 2016 and the rise of extreme white nationalists in the US and Europe, understanding the term 'fascism' has taken on a new urgency as well, but far better historical analysis and comparative detail are required. A far better understanding is also required of the *political economy* of fascism historically.

The upheavals of 1919, I believe, were connected in global ways that continue to have relevance and a disturbing presence in our own time. We ignore at our own peril the history and the global dynamics of that past and how it reaches into our present.

Notes

1 The scholarly and popular literature on specific events and specific countries that occurred in 1919 is vast, but broader global syntheses of this history specific to 1919, dealing with both 'East' (Asia) and 'West' (Europe and America), are surprisingly sparse. For a well-researched popular narrative, see William K. Klingaman, *1919: The Year Our World Began* (New York: St Martin's Press, 1987). For scholarly work, perhaps the best recent economic history (spanning the Great War to the Great Depression but with a crucial focus on the years around 1919) is Adam Tooze, *The Deluge: The Great War and the Remaking of Global Order* (London: Penguin, 2014).

2 The most work in this area has been in German Third Reich business histories, the most important being those of Peter Hayes, *Industry and Ideology: IG Farben in the Nazi Era* (Cambridge University Press, 2001), and Hayes, *From Cooperation to Complicity: Degussa in the Third Reich* (Cambridge University Press, 2006). While historians writing in English on German businesses under the Third Reich have focused mainly on single corporations, for Italian fascism the only major business history is Franklin Hugh Adler, *Italian Industrialists from Liberalism to Fascism: The Political Development of the Industrial Bourgeoisie, 1906–1934* (Cambridge University Press), which focuses on industrial associations rather than particular companies. Hayes' sources are company documents released with company agreement following the settlement of foreign forced labour claims that involved years of international negotiations with Third Reich era companies, the German and Austrian governments, and all major Allied powers that were affected by Nazi foreign forced labour. Adler uses industrial association sources, but in contrast to Hayes takes the story back to the 1900s. Hayes has primarily an institutional focus on management views, while Adler's focus is on the changing ideological character of business executives. No comparable studies for Japanese companies or industrial association under imperial fascism exist in English, and to my knowledge none comparable to the scholarship on European businesses and fascism exist in Japanese. The major Japanese *zaibatsu* were central to war production during the Pacific War (1937–1945), and during World War II (1941–1945) led the government production committees, paradoxically similar to how American business leaders did the same under the Roosevelt administration's wartime production drive. While both Germany and Austria have acknowledged the crimes of foreign forced labour under the Third Reich and have settled financial claims litigated by survivors, Japan continues to refuse to acknowledge widespread foreign forced labour of Koreans and Chinese, claiming all settlements were made with South Korea in the 1965 peace treaty and that Koreans and Chinese working in Japan were 'conscripted' legally, not forced or coerced against their will. As of this writing, Mitsubishi's refusal to make payments of unpaid wages mandated by the South Korean Supreme Court to former Korean forced labourers and families where labourers have died, and the Mitsubishi refusal having the full support of the Abe LDP government, has led to a full scale trade war between South Korea and Japan. For background on the South Korean Supreme Court case, see David Palmer, 'Foreign forced labor at Mitsubishi's Nagasaki and Hiroshima Shipyards: Big business, militarized government, and the absence of shipbuilding workers' rights in World War II Japan,' in Marcel van der Linden and Magaly Rodriguez Garcia (eds), *On*

Coerced Labour: Work and Compulsion after Chattel Slavery (Leiden: Brill, 2016), 159–84.

3 An immense number of works cover the origins of the Nazi Party and Hitler, which need not be cited in this short analysis. The same is true of European fascism beyond Nazism. Michael Mann, *Fascists* (Cambridge: Cambridge University Press, 2004) provides a country-by-country overview of fascist forces in Italy, Germany, Austria, Hungary, Romania, and Spain. It is valuable as a comparative study with a sociological perspective, but only touches briefly on events after World War I. More detailed historical studies provide a closer view of events in the 1919 era. For Germany, see William A. Pelz, *The Spartakusbund and the German Working Class Movement, 1914–1919* (Lewiston, NY: Edwin Mellen Press, 1987); and F.L. Carsten, *Revolution in Central Europe, 1918–1919* (London: Temple Smith, 1972), which also covers Austria and Hungary. For Italy, see Gwyn A. Williams, *Proletarian Order: Antonio Gramsci, Factory Councils and the Origins of Communism in Italy, 1911–1921* (London: Pluto Press, 1975); R.J.B. Bosworth, *Mussolini's Italy* (London: Allen Lane, 2005), 93–149. For Hungary, see Rudolf L. Tokes, *Bela Kun and the Hungarian Soviet Republic: The Origins and Role of the Communist Party of Hungary in the Revolutions of 1918–1919* (New York: Frederick A. Praeger, 1967); Peter Pastor, ed., *Revolutions and Interventions in Hungary and Its Neighbor States, 1918–1919* (New York: Columbia University Press, 1988).

4 Ann Hagedorn, *Savage Peace: Hope and Fear in America, 1919* (New York: Simon & Schuster, 2007) is a detailed narrative of these American conflicts and social conditions. On labour struggles, Philip S. Foner, *History of the Labor Movement in the United States, Vol. 8: Postwar Struggles, 1918–1920* (New York: International Publishers, 1988) is a useful national survey, although superseded by more detailed and analytically more sophisticated studies. The steel strike is covered well in David Brody, *Labor in Crisis: The Steel Strike of 1919* (Urbana: University of Illinois Press, 1987, originally published 1965). For leftwing strike organizing, which includes the steel strike and meatpackers' strike in Chicago, see Edward P. Johanningsmeir, *Forging American Communism: The Life of William Z. Foster* (Princeton: Princeton University Press, 1997), 111–74. The first general strike that took over an entire city government is covered in Harvey O'Connor, *Revolution in Seattle: A Memoir* (Seattle: Left Bank Books, 1981, originally published 1964). For the race riots and crisis faced by African Americans in 1919, see William M. Tuttle, *Race Riot: Chicago in the Red Summer of 1919* (New York: Athenium, 1970); and David Levering Lewis, *W.E.B. Du Bois: The Fight for Equality and the American Century, 1919–1963* (New York: Henry Holt, 2000) for the connection of the 1919 upheavals and the rise of the NAACP and modern civil rights movement over subsequent decades. For the Red Scare, William Preston, Jr., *Aliens and Dissenters: Federal Suppression of Radicals, 1903–1933* (Urbana: University of Illinois Press, 1994).

5 Chow Tse-tsung, *The May Fourth Movement: Intellectual Revolution in Modern China* (Cambridge, MA: Harvard University Press, 1960); Vera Schwarcz, *The Chinese Enlightenment: Intellectuals and the Legacy of the May Fourth Movement of 1919* (Berkeley: University of California Press, 1986).

6 Gloria Davies, *Lu Hsun's Revolution: Writings in a Time of Violence* (Cambridge, MA: Harvard University Press, 2013), 126, 127.

7 Michael D. Shin, *Korean National Identity under Japanese Colonial Rule: Yi Gwang-su and the March First Movement of 1919* (London: Routledge, 2018); Hildi Kang, *Under the Black Umbrella: Voices from Colonial Korea, 1910–1945* (Ithaca, NY: Cornell University Press, 2001); Chong-sik Lee, *The Politics of Korean Nationalism* (Berkeley: University of California Press, 1963).

8 Mao Tse-tung, 'The May 4th Movement,' in *Selected Works of Mao Tse-tung, Vol. II* (Beijing: Foreign Languages Press, 1967), 237–9.

9 Peter Duus, *The Abacus and the Sword: The Japanese Penetration of Korea, 1895–1910* (Berkeley: University of California Press, 1995).

10 Alexis Dudden, *Japan's Colonization of Korea: Discourse and Power* (Honolulu: University of Hawai'i Press, 2005).

11 John G. Roberts, *Mitsui: Three Centuries of Japanese Business* (NY: Weatherhill, 1975); H. Morikawa, 'The Organizational Structure of Mitsubishi and Mitsui Zaibatsu, 1868–1922,' *Business History Review* 44, No. 1 (1970). For the origin of Mitsubishi and its rise as a modern corporation based heavily on military production by the 1910s and 1920s using the example of Nagasaki, see David Palmer, 'Nagasaki's Districts: Western Contact with Japan through the History of a City's Space,' *Journal of Urban History* Vol. 42, No. 3 (2016): 477–505. There are no comprehensive histories of Mitsubishi in English. A key source in Japanese in the company history, Mitsubishi, *Mitsubishi jyūkōgyō kabushiki kaishashi* (*The History of Mitsubishi Heavy Industries*) (Tokyo: Mitsubishi, 1956), which covers the heavy industry division in detail from origin to the 1950s, including all plants, employment numbers, products such as ship lists, and managerial structures and changes. This contrasts with the numerous histories of Nazi era big businesses that are in English or English translation. The Japanese World War II wartime economy is virtually unexplored by scholars publishing in English, leaving a huge gap in our knowledge of the relationship of big business to Japanese imperial fascism and the origins of military fascism.

12 F.L. Carsten, *The Rise of Fascism* (Berkeley: University of California Press, 1971), 9.

13 Tooze, *Deluge*, 170.

14 One of the best analyses of this relationship is Adler, *Italian Industrialists from Liberalism to Fascism*. Adler delves into the ideology of industrial business executives using industry association sources. He argues that they actively took part in the emerging ideology of fascism rather than moving toward it in response to the strike movements of 1919 and later years, as the forces that united around Mussolini by the early 1920s had already destroyed the capacity of resistance by unions and workers' political parties. One could apply a similar ideological trend among American business leaders that culminated in the triumph of the far right in the modern Republican Party in an era when trade unions represented only a very small percentage of the US workforce. A similar pattern is evident in the case of Japan, with industrialists uniting behind the non-radical military imperial fascists in power represented by types like Tojo. The case of Germany, however, is quite different given the extreme level of conflict between strong left wing workers' political groups and the Nazis prior to Hitler being appointed Chancellor. Nevertheless, Hitler's violent purge of the radical anti-business S.A. does indicate a similar pattern. Nazi Germany required the full cooperation of big business, which in turn gained huge profits from the new regime.

15 See Alfred D. Chandler, Jr., *Scale and Scope: The Dynamics of Industrial Capitalism* (Cambridge, Mass.: Harvard University Press, 1990), 11, 12, 503–7, 534, 535; and Chandler, *The Visible Hand: The Managerial Revolution in American Business* (Cambridge, Mass.: Harvard University Press, 1977). Chandler considers the British version as *personal capitalism*. One might say that Japan was a kind of hybrid of variants – German for its cooperative (but internal) methods; American for its competitive approach to rival *zaibatsu*; and British to a degree given the role of family ownership at the top, but with professional managers in decision-making, unlike the British. *Zaibatsu* followed the classic, but relatively true, clichés about Japanese culture: group decisions, conformity to authority, loyalty to the 'family' / institution one belongs to. In this sense the Japanese big company was most like the German big company, but without the direct dominance of the leading authority – in Japan the dominance was more subtle and indirect, even if the authority was revered.

16 For Japanese imperial fascism, this three tier labour system is described in Palmer, 'Foreign forced labor at Mitsubishi's Nagasaki and Hiroshima Shipyards'. Nazi Germany followed a similar labour system that was used in state and private businesses (Auschwitz, for example, had both a death camp and an industrial production camp, the latter operated by private company I.G.) While the Japanese did work Koreans to death in coal mines, deliberate extermination was not the regime's goal, as was the case with this Nazi practice toward Jewish workers.

17 I view the South during the decades of racial segregation as a prototype of possible American fascism. White authorities and vigilantes ruled through terror against African Americans and any of their white supporters; imposed segregation laws to enforce that terror; prevented voting, equal education, access to public facilities; and imposed economic peonage through sharecropping and extreme debt imposition.

18 Douglas A. Blackmon, *Slavery by Another Name: The Re-enslavement of Black Americans from the Civil War to World War II* (New York: Anchor Books, 2008) covers the economic oppression of African Americans in the post-Civil War South through the proto-fascist Southern segregationist system, enforced through terror and state control. The historiography on the post-Civil War American South and African Americans is massive. Representative works include Roy E. Finkenbine, ed., *Sources of the African American Past: Primary Sources in American History* (New York, Pearson Longman, 2004), 96–117; Herbert Shapiro, *White Violence and Black Resistance: From Reconstruction to Montgomery* (Amherst, 1988); and C. Vann Woodward, *The Strange Career of Jim Crow* (New York: Oxford University Press, 1974), a classic historical analysis that views full scale racial segregation based on changes of Southern state's constitutional law starting in the 1890s and a direct consequence of African American disfranchisement. This loss of voting was enforced by white terror against those who continued to try to register to vote. America's racial segregation served as a model for Hitler, as documented in James Q. Whitman, *Hitler's American Model: The United States and the Making of American Race Law* (Princeton University Press, 2017).

Belgium, 1919

Joseph Cardijn begins the Young Christian Workers Movement

VAL NOONE

In 1919, following his release from jail for patriotic activities, a 37-year-old Flemish priest in Belgium named Joseph Cardijn and his lay collaborators began a movement which became Jeunesse Ouvrière Chrétienne (Young Christian Workers). This paper outlines the pre-history of the YCW; its formation and subsequent worldwide influence including its role in the Second Vatican Council; and its growth in Australia in the 1940s through the 1960s, in part as an alternative to the undiscriminating anti-communism of the Santamaria Movement. A short reflection is offered on Catholic-Communist interaction, plus a note on current Australian research.

***

If some felt in 1919 that things were falling apart, others such as Joseph Cardijn and his collaborators in Belgium were full of energy for building a peaceful and just world. Here are seven snapshots of how they started a church-based youth movement with working-class characteristics, which spread around the world.

Joseph Cardijn in the 1950s: 'Every young worker is worth more than a pot of gold'. Melbourne YCW Archive.

Cardijn in World War I

In 1915, in November, the month for special prayers for the dead, in the great cathedral of Saint Gudule in Brussels, Cardinal Désiré Mercier, an outstanding figure in the Belgian resistance to German military occupation, presided over a packed solemn service for military and civilian victims of the war. The preacher at the cathedral was the brilliant 33-year-old Father Joseph Cardijn, a Flemish-speaker who grew up poor in Halle in central Belgium, director of social action in the archdiocese. Cardijn denounced the unjust German aggression and described the conduct of those collaborating with the Germans as 'prostitution'.[1]

Meanwhile Australian soldiers were on their way to Belgium. Lord Horatio Kitchener, the British secretary of state for war, responsible for the Gallipoli campaign, was about to inspect Gallipoli and accept defeat and withdrawal, which would in turn mean the Anzacs going to fight in Belgium and France. Indeed, many Australians had enlisted because they were told they were going to defend Belgium. By strange coincidence, among the soldiers' children and grandchildren an important minority would, in time, join a youth organisation inspired by this Belgian priest.

The following November, Cardijn publicly supported Mercier, and other Belgian leaders, in a formal protest to the Central Powers and to the Pope against the deportation of Belgian workers into Germany for the munitions factories. This time Cardijn spoke in the name of 130,000 members of the Christian Trade Unions. As a result he served six months in the prison of St Gilles. In June 1918 Cardijn was back at St Gilles, this time with 10 years hard labour for his part in setting up an observation post monitoring munitions trains and notifying the Allies but was released following the signing of the Armistice. In his notes Cardijn recorded:

> A prisoner's cell is never empty. It is filled with all the visons of the ideal which is the content and pursuit of his life. What makes prison bearable is the passionate desire and ardent hope of getting back into harness next day.[2]

Cardijn and comrades smuggled letters in and out of the jail. He wrote talks for workers' groups and guides for their study circles and enquiry programs. He re-read the Bible and several works of Karl Marx including Das Kapital. Sixty years after the Communist Manifesto and the International Workingmen's Association a new form of Christian solidarity with the workers' movements was coming into being.

A few years later when he was writing the manual for the Jeunesse Ouvrière Chrétienne, the Young Christian Workers, Cardijn worked from his prison notebooks. One biography calls it 'a providential imprisonment'.[3]

La Jeunesse Syndicaliste

One hundred years ago, during the northern summer of 1919, Cardijn and associates founded an organisation called La Jeunesse Syndicaliste (Young Trade Unionists). Freed from jail, Cardijn – who had sworn by the bed of his dying father that he would dedicate himself to the working class and who was a friend to school mates who went to the mines and mills as he went to the seminary – turned his native enormous energy to what he saw as his life's work: forming groups of young workers who could tackle the problems of young workers. The Belgian church had previously taken aspects of the workers' problems seriously but in a paternalistic manner under middle-class leadership linked in politics to the conservative Catholic Party.

Cardijn promoted leaders who were self-reliant young workers. Three are famous for their collaboration with him in 1919: Fernand Tonnet, returned from the front, Paul Garcet from Laeken and Jacques Meert, a young iron worker from nearby Schaerbeek. Conservatives started a rival group under the old middle-class umbrella but in vain: with Mercier's assistance La Jeunesse Syndicaliste found a headquarters. Cardijn was afflicted with tuberculosis and went to Cannes on the Riviera where he recuperated.

A young plasterer Jan Schellekens organised 40 of them to start a newspaper, Jeunesse Syndicaliste. In the upsurge of labour militancy after the war, and after the success of the Bolshevik revolution, this group made an important contribution, joining forces with the Women's Social Action run by Victoire Cappe and Maria Baers and the journal, La Femme Belge (The Belgian Woman), as well a group of young intellectuals. In 1924 they changed their name to Jeunesse Ouvrière Chrétienne (JOC), the Young Christian Workers (YCW). From the French initials JOC, the YCW method is often referred to as Jocist.

The following year, in a dramatic move that launched Cardijn on to a world stage, Pope Pius XI gave enthusiastic endorsement to the JOC. Cardijn often told the story of that moment: 'Here at last' said the Pope, 'is someone who speaks to me about the masses! The greatest scandal of the nineteenth century was the loss of the workers to the Church. The Church needs the workers and the workers need the Church.'[4] Cardijn told this story on his visits to Australia in 1959 and 1966.

The militant Cardijn became shrewder and diplomatic as he and the other founders used official church structures to build the movement. Before looking at some forerunners of the YCW, let us note with respect that both Tonnet and Garcet died in Dachau.

Needleworkers of Laeken

The mention of Victoire Cappe is a reminder of an important factor in the formation of the Jeunesse Syndicaliste and the YCW: Cardijn began with women's groups. Kiara Gigacz has recently drawn attention to Cappe's neglected influence on Cardijn, including around 1913 when he was stationed in the parish of Our Lady's, Laeken.[5] Given pastoral duties with the Girls' Guild, Cardijn not only promoted religious practices but also set up study circles of working women and apprentices. With mentoring by Cappe, a dedicated feminist and known for her work with the Needleworkers' Union, the girls formed trade unions for laundry workers, seamstresses and domestics. A women's league built up membership of 1,000, with a school of cutting and sewing, an employment agency, and also a strong program of church attendance. One of those mentored by Cappe, Madeleine de Roo became a prominent leader of the women's YCW along with Marguerite Fievez.

19th-century forerunners

Cardijn belongs in a line of Catholic radicals who during the industrial revolution, against huge odds, attempted to keep or take the church into solidarity with the working class.[6] For instance, his father had been involved with the group around Father Adolf Daens who was dismissed by the hierarchy for his political commitment to the workers. Taken as a youngster by his father to hear Daens, Cardijn drew some tactical lessons from Daens' defeat. The harsh conditions for working people into which Cardijn and the YCW were born have been portrayed strikingly in two films, Daens and Germinal, both of which are set near Cardijn's birthplace, one in Belgium and the other, based on Emile Zola's novel, in northern France. Then as a theology student, Cardijn became an enthusiastic supporter of Marc Sangnier who in 1894 had founded a democratic and anti-imperialist Catholic lay group in France called Le Sillon (The Furrow). This broke up under the pressure of a ban by the church hierarchy.

In his recent doctoral thesis Stefan Gigacz has detailed other European Catholic thinkers who were important to Cardijn and his circle. One example was Hugues-Felicité de Lamennais (1782–1854), a Catholic priest who challenged a conservative church allied with the rich and sought a return to the Gospels and a new alliance with the poor. In 1830 he and others founded the newspaper, L'Avenir (The Future), which called for the separation of church and state and for freedom of conscience. In the next couple of years the Pope and the hierarchy condemned de Lamennais and drove him out of the church.

Two other examples of historical influences on Cardijn will suffice: Alphonse Gratry (1805–1872) and Léon Ollé-Laprune (1839–1898), both of whom continued the de Lamennais spirit of a this-worldly religion.

Gratry wrote a series of influential books which encouraged people to 'read the signs of the times', draw conclusions about what needed change and join the movements for social improvement. Cardijn studied them and Gigacz finds in Gratry the basis of a slogan Cardijn used to sum up the method he was teaching young workers, namely See, Judge, Act. As Ollé-Laprune later emphasised, Gratry 'signals the hideous wounds' of society.

Achille Liénart, a pioneer chaplain to the YCW and later a leading reforming cardinal at the Second Vatican Council, gave credit to Cardijn for serious study of 'all the previous movements, their insights and their weaknesses'. This was a key to his canny diplomacy with the hierarchy.

Growth including a role in Vatican II

By the end of the 1930s the YCW had spread around Europe, into Latin America, Canada, Australia and Indochina but only a little into the United States. In 1957 delegates to the YCW's first world council in Rome filled St Peter's square. The high point of the influence of Cardijn and the Jocist movements on official Church policy came in the positive declarations of the Second Vatican Council (1961–1965) on the church and the modern world. Gigacz's thesis presents a strong case for this claim. 'Despite Cardijn's absence from the drafting process, through the work of the Jocist bishops and periti, the Cardijn dialectic emerged as the foundation of Gaudium et Spes,' he concluded. That is, the crucial Council declaration on the Church in the modern world incorporated many aspects of Cardijn's philosophy, particularly regarding the vocation of the Christian to build a better world.[7]

From 1940: the Australian section

An outline of YCW history in Australia: The Catholic bishops first officially recognised and funded the YCW on 10 October 1940 in Melbourne with a national brief. In the mid-1930s Kevin Kelly, then in his twenties, a family friend of Australian Labor Party leader James Scullin, and also active in

Melbourne Catholic university circles, had read and circulated materials from the French and later Belgian YCW. From 1936 the Catholic Worker newspaper, at the time edited by Bartholomew Santamaria and managed by Frank Keating, publicised reports about Cardijn and the European YCW. For a couple of years from 1937 Father Frank Lombard, 27, experimented with elements of YCW methods in the parish of St Joseph's Northcote. In 1940 Lombard took on the dual role of part-time army chaplain and also chaplain to the newly formed Melbourne YCW. Since then, the organisation itself has produced study guides, pamphlets and magazines which are invaluable in documenting its history. Lombard was, in his way, Australia's Cardijn. Early lay leaders included Leo Tyrell, Frank McCann, Ted Long and Kevin Toomey.[8] The initial program of the Australian YCW reflected the widespread hopes for a more just society towards the end of World War II, a mood that Cardijn and his team exemplified in 1919.[9]

The 1940s and 1950s were years of dramatic expansion throughout the dioceses of Australia, excepting Sydney, with thousands of branch members in hundreds of parish groups, many leaders' groups and large sports competitions. Girls groups had a different name initially, National Catholic Girls' Movement. Apart from parish groups some larger activities were organised such as holiday camps and, for five years beginning in 1941, a series of big youth rallies at Xavier College. A newspaper called New Youth began around 1945 and lasted more than 20 years. Its banner read: 'A new youth for a new Australia'. Frank McCann went to work for the first YCW cooperative trading society. A men's extension committee was formed which helped in setting up a hostel at Albert Park, a holiday camp at Phillip Island, an office building in Lonsdale Street, training schools at Maiya Wamba, Cheltenham, and Lowanna, Brighton. By 1955 there were 5000 members in 17 Australian dioceses. Representatives went to international meetings in Brussels, Rome, Singapore, Manila and New Delhi; Cardijn visited Australia in 1959 and 1966. Cardijn's influence spread beyond YCW, for example, to Catholic intellectuals in the Newman Society.[10] From the 1970s Australian YCW has declined for reasons which need analysis on another occasion.

The YCW method in Australia was based on a twofold approach: a leaders' group which met weekly for reflection on the gospels and life, and for planning; and sporting teams, dances and other social functions for general members. While handbooks for groups pointed towards conducting discussions of workers' problems, in practice, parish groups pursued associated aims such as building Catholic community cohesion, improving Mass attendance, teaching Catholic morality and fostering Catholic marriages. In organising social junctions YCW faced opposition from the existing, and in its day thriving, Catholic Young Men's Society. Due to this conflict YCW membership in Melbourne was originally confined to the 14–18-year-old group.

YCW had more serious differences with Santamaria and the Movement he ran.[11] At the time Santamaria was working for the Catholic bishops in an organisation called the Australian National Secretariat of Catholic Action. In short, he wanted the YCW to be a recruiting ground for his secret cells in the trade union movement and the ALP. While Lombard and the YCW lay leaders shared an anti-communist outlook, they regarded Santamaria's clandestine tactics as mistaken. Also Santamaria ran his organisation from the top down whereas, true to Cardijn's teachings, the Australian YCW believed in local young workers taking their own initiatives.

Historian Edmund Campion remarked that Cardijn's 'whole-hearted acceptance of the working-class ethos shocked some of the middle class'.[12] The spirit of the movement is conveyed by the YCW prayer used at the opening of meetings:

> Lord Jesus, A Worker like me, Help me, and all my fellow workers, to think like You, to work with You, to pray through You, to live in You, to give You all my strength and all my time. May Your Kingdom come in all our factories, farms, workshops, offices, and in all our homes. Be everywhere better known, better loved, better served. Deliver us forever from injustice and hatred, from evil and sin. May our souls

> remain in Your Grace today, and may the soul of every worker who died on labour's battlefield rest in peace. Amen.

Of the many points in the YCW prayer, the one that strikes many hearers as exceptional is the call for solidarity with 'every worker who died on labour's battlefield'. Peter Robinson who was in the Malvern YCW in the early 1950s recalled the impact of the opening words, 'Dear Jesus, a worker like me'. He said the 'young blokes said this prayer at every meeting and they really believed it. It was very significant.'[13] This handful of paragraphs take us a few short steps along the long road to an overview of the Australian YCW.

'Negative anti-communism is doing nothing'

Catholics, Communists and Cardijn: The YCW had an ambiguous task. Partly it was an official Catholic organisation with a mission to bring workers to church, partly it was an organisation of young workers struggling to do away with the injustices facing them. The YCW set out to both bring about justice for the working class and also to convert the working class to Jesus Christ. Speaking in 1948, Cardijn outlined the characteristics of modern industrial working conditions and argued that 'the workers' problem' (Cardijn's phrase for all the issues facing the industrial working class) had to be taken seriously by Christians and that it existed separately of agitation by communists and socialists. He emphasised the global nature of the economy and the need for international consciousness and action by workers. He based his case on the dignity of every young worker which derived from God's plan, and he wanted the YCW to be educative, apostolic and missionary. He said that, 'A negative attitude is a death-blow to the Church. To be merely anti-Communist or anti-Socialist is doing nothing.'[14]

In general, the Australian YCW adopted Cardijn's view. It aimed to tackle the problems of young workers in a spirit of reform, making important contributions in areas such as apprenticeship conditions, credit and finance through its cooperatives and later to road safety with its successful seatbelts campaign. While avowing that it did not seek competition, conflicts with communists were part and parcel of the early years. In July 1945 YCW spoke against what it called 'the communist youth racket' led, it claimed, by the International Youth Committee in Sydney. A particular target of their concerns was the Eureka Youth League.[15] Yet YCW was looking for a positive way forward and, at times, was conciliatory. New Youth claimed that 'hate and violence' only harmed the workers. According to their reporter,

> to listen to the Reds, you would think no one else except themselves was doing anything. We know, we work in factories and shops. Our eyes and ears are just as wide open as those of any Red. We Young Christian Workers are just as desperately anxious for a change as the most idealistic Moscow-man.[16]

Writing about the French YCW in these same years, Oscar Arnal argued that, from a Marxist perspective, the YCW's links with the hierarchy resulted in bishops urging workers towards harmony with bosses.[17] He further judged that although, at times, YCW played down class conflict it was at all times committed to democratic social reforms. In Australia, this orientation made it a constructive alternative to the undiscriminating anti-communism of the Santamaria Movement.

Historiographical note

To conclude these seven snapshots of YCW history here is a note about the current state of Australian research. Although no overall history of the Australian YCW has been published, in the early 1980s David Kehoe wrote a commissioned history which remains unpublished after key founders judged that his manuscript, though valuable, did not adequately reflect their experiences. As noted above, several writers have discussed the YCW's crucial opposition to the Movement style of Catholicism. However, Brian Burke has stressed the importance of telling the YCW story according to its own rhythms, and of not defining the YCW by its opposition to the Santamaria influence.[18] Indeed, Edmund Campion, John Maguire, Breda Phillips, Margaret Press, Hugh O'Sullivan, myself and others have written about the Australian YCW in ways that accord with Burke's observation.[19] And, as indicated, Stefan Gigacz has broken new ground in the history of the International YCW.

In 2014 a group who hold the funds left over from properties owned in the YCW's heyday invested money in a dual history project under the direction of Bill Armstrong and Melissa Walsh: the collection and digitisation of available YCW archives around Australia, for example, minutes, study guides and pamphlets; conducting 41 interviews, which are now digitised and transcribed.[20] While State Library of Victoria will be home to this valuable archive, a working group of which I am a member is looking to make it more accessible by providing a timeline, a glossary of important terms such as See-Judge-Act, and Catholic Action, and a biographical register of key people.

Notes

1 These paragraphs are based on Michael de la Bedoyère, *The Cardijn Story* (London: Longmans, 1958), 54 ff. Marguerite Fievez, Jacques Meert and Roger Aubert, *Cardijn*, translated by Edward Mitchinson with a Preface by Dom Helder Camara (London: Young Christian Workers, 1974), 39 ff.

2 *Cardijn*, 41.

3 Ibid., 37.

4 Eugene Langdale (ed.) *Challenge to Action: Addresses of Monsignor Joseph Cardijn* (Melbourne: Geoffrey Chapman, 1955). See Langdale's 'Introduction' 11.

5 Kiara Gigacz, 'Victoire Cappe, Cardijn and the See, Judge, Act', talk given at Conference on 'Formation, Laity & Vatican II: the YCW in Australia', Catholic Theological College, Melbourne 29 July 2017.

6 Stefan Robert Gigacz, 'The leaven and the Council: Joseph Cardijn and the Jocist

networks at Vatican II', PhD thesis, University of Divinity Melbourne, 2018.

7 Gigacz, chapter 9 passim.

8 This and following paragraphs are based on Val Noone, 'A new youth for a new Australia: an Australian religious youth group of the 1960s', *Footprints*, journal of Melbourne Diocesan Historical Commission, December 1995, 20–42. 'Special issue on the history of the YCW: 1', *Footprints*, 29.2 (Dec. 2014), edited by David Moloney assisted by Rachel Naughton; contributors: David Kehoe, Max Vodola, Bruce Duncan, Peter Price, Melissa Walsh, Rachel Naughton. 'Special issue on the history of the YCW: 2', *Footprints*, 30.1 (June 2015), edited by David Moloney assisted by Rachel Naughton; contributors; Guido Vogels, Race Mathews, Helen Praetz, Kevin Peoples, John McKinnon, John Finlayson, Denis Sheehan. David Kehoe, 'Kevin Thomas Kelly: prophet of the Australian YCW', in Stefan Gigacz (ed.), Cardijn Studies, Vol. 1, No, 1 (June 2017), 1–12. John Molony, *Towards an Apostolic Laity* (Melbourne: Young Christian Workers, 1960).

9 'YCW's 15-point programme for young workers', 'National committee appointed: four states represented', 'Youth speaks on youth problems: Australian Youth Committee conference reviewed', *New Youth*, No. 2 (July 1944).

10 Vincent Buckley, *Cutting Green Hay* (Melbourne: Penguin, 1983), passim.

11 Paul Ormonde, *The Movement* (Melbourne: Nelson, 1972), 50, 55, 100. B.A. Santamaria, *Against the Tide* (Melbourne: Oxford University Press, 1981), 156–8. Bruce Duncan, *Crusade or Conspiracy? Catholics and the Anti-communist Struggle in Australia* (Sydney: UNSW Press, 2001), passim. Gerard Henderson, *Mr Santamaria and the Bishops* (Sydney: Studies in the Christian Movement, 1982), 28.

12 Edmund Campion, *Rockchoppers* (Melbourne: Penguin, 1982), 190.

13 Denis Sheehan, 'Interview with Peter Robinson', 25 September 2014.

14 *The Cardijn Story*, 61.

15 'Faked world youth conference', *New Youth*, May 1946, 1.

16 'Hate and violence only harms workers: We're not competing with the Communists', 'YCW national conference Brisbane', *New Youth*, No. 11 (August 1945), 1.

17 Oscar Arnal, *Priests in Working-Class Blue: the History of the Worker-Priests (1943–1954)* (New York: Paulist Press, 1986), 29.

18 Val Noone, 'Santamaria years: a YCW view, an interview with Brian Burke', *Táin*, No. 31 (June–July 2004), 18–20.

19 Campion, Rockchoppers. John Maguire, *Prologue: a History of the Catholic Church as Seen from Townsville 1863–1983* (Toowoomba: Church Archivists' Society, 1990). Val Noone, *Disturbing the War: Melbourne Catholics and Vietnam* (Melbourne: Spectrum, 1993). Breda Phillips, *More Prophetic Than We Knew: a history of the YCW in the diocese of Sandhurst* (Bendigo: published by the author, 1999). Margaret Press, *Colour and Shadow: South Australian Catholics, 1906–1962* (Adelaide: Archdiocese of Adelaide, 1991). Hugh O'Sullivan, *The Clatter of Wooden Clogs; a challenge for today's young worker* (Sydney: Australian Young Christian Workers, 1991).

20 'YCW archival documents and jpgs' and 'YCW interviews transcripts', digital files held by Australian YCW, Melbourne.

Relativity and Reconciliation in the Aftermath of War

RODERICK W. HOME*

Science, its practitioners have been wont to declare, is not bounded by nationality or culture. Its subject-matter, the natural world, is universal, and the subject's development depends on the free interchange of information between scientists who from the point of view of their profession are citizens not of this or that nation-state but of a wider republic of letters. So, at least, we have been assured; some of you will remember the huge ruckus that ensued in this country a generation ago, using precisely this kind of language, when the Fraser Government barred a delegate from the Soviet Union from entering Australia to attend a major international scientific congress.[1] And for much of its history, science does seem to have operated in this way.

Almost sixty years ago, a leading English biologist, Sir Gavan De Beer, who also had a well-developed interest in the history of science, published a documentary history entitled *The Sciences Were Never at War* that dealt

* This paper does not pretend to embody original research. For historians of science, at least, the story told is well known and there is a very extensive literature about it on which, in the context of a symposium focusing on the events of the year 1919, I have drawn in order to bring the story before an audience less likely to be familiar with it.

with the relations between French and British science and scientists during the 18th and early 19th centuries, a period during which France and Britain were almost continuously at war.[2] Despite such hostilities, the documents published by De Beer showed that contact between the scientists of the two nations was seldom interrupted and, even when it was, this was only ever a very temporary thing. A remarkable incident that De Beer documented concerned the French botanist Jacques-Julien Labillardière, one of the scientists who accompanied Bruny d'Entrecasteaux on his famous voyage in the early 1790s in search of the missing explorer Lapérouse, who collected botanical specimens assiduously at all the expedition's Australian landfalls. The expedition, having failed to find any trace of Lapérouse, suffered various calamities on the voyage home, including the death of its commander, dissention among the officers and scientific staff between monarchists and supporters of the Revolution, detention by the Dutch authorities in Batavia and, eventually, capture by a British warship leading to the seizure of Labillardière's collections and his being carried to England as a prisoner of war, along with the rest of the surviving ship's complement. Once in England, however, things looked up for Labillardière. He was never incarcerated and was eventually allowed to return to France; most importantly, thanks to the intervention of Joseph Banks who explicitly made appeal to the ideal of the republic of letters in arguing Labillardière's case, he was allowed to take his enormously valuable collection of natural history specimens back to France with him, on the basis of which he wrote the first extended account of the Australian flora.[3]

The First World War, however, to a large extent put paid to these notions about the internationalism of science. In part, this reflected the fact that science was beginning to be valued as a potential contributor to a nation's war effort, so that the scientists themselves began to see themselves as an integral part of that effort. Of course, even in the French Revolutionary wars in the 1790s, the successes of the French army had owed much to the work of the chemist Antoine Lavoisier in bolstering both the quantity and quality of its gunpowder; but in the First World War the contributions of scientists on both sides in support of their armed services was on a vastly greater scale. Think, for example, of the work of Fritz Haber on the fixation of atmospheric nitrogen to make ammonia, fundamental to the German stockpiling of explosives and fertilizer without which their war effort would soon have ground to a halt; or of his later work on poison gas, chlorine at first and later mustard gas.[4] On the Allied side, think of the army of chemists from all over the British Empire, including Australia, who were recruited to staff the munitions factories that supplied the ever-expanding needs of the military;[5] or of the invention of ASDIC to detect enemy submarines;[6] or of the successful development by the Adelaide-born Nobel-prizewinner Lawrence Bragg of sound-ranging as a means of pinpointing and so targeting the enemy's big guns on the Western Front.[7]

There is, however, more to the story than this. Beyond the new recognition, by both themselves and others, that their work could contribute in such very practical ways on the actual battlefield, many scientists on both sides during the First World War seem to have been swept up by the warlike fervour of the day, and to have responded in an emotional way to what was happening around them. And it was this, I believe, rather than the more concrete contributions of the scientists to the prosecution of the war, that led to the tensions that beset the world's scientific community in the post-war years and that form the essential backdrop to the story I want to tell here.

Before I take up that theme, though, let me introduce the principal character in my story, Albert Einstein. His name, of course, needs no introduction – indeed, how it came to be a household word around the world is part of the story – but I need to say something about the man himself, and about the work he did in the decade leading up to the outbreak of war, and then during the war itself.[8]

The story has often been told of how, in 1905, when the young Einstein, not long out of university, was employed as an examining clerk in the patents office in Bern, in Switzerland, and thinking about physics in the evenings, he published three remarkable papers in what was then the world's leading physics journal, *Annalen der Physik*. He also successfully submitted his PhD thesis, published in *Annalen der Physik* early in 1906, to the University of Zürich, that also included ground-breaking work which, interestingly enough, was done completely independently of, but at almost the same moment as, work done by William Sutherland here in Melbourne, in which exactly the same results were arrived at, by the same route.[9] While this fourth paper of Einstein's was to become the most frequently cited of all his papers because the fundamental equation that he derived in it proved to have widespread practical application, it was the papers published during the preceding few months that made him famous. One of these was the iconic paper in which Einstein announced his so-called special theory of relativity, the follow-up to which I'll be pursuing in a moment. However, to illustrate the level of achievement that we're talking about here, I should point out that when Einstein was awarded the Nobel Prize for physics in 1922, it wasn't for his work on relativity theory but for his work in one of the other 1905 papers, work in which he successfully explained various puzzling features of the photoelectric effect – the ejection of electrons from metal surfaces by ultraviolet radiation – by assuming that the radiation travelled in packets ('quanta') rather than as a continuous wave as everyone for very good reason had long believed.[10] And the third paper had almost as great an impact at the time. In this paper Einstein demonstrated the physical reality of atoms – still at that time a matter of considerable dispute – by showing how Brownian motion, the apparently random motions of microscopic particles suspended in a fluid, could be accounted for, in full quantitative detail, in terms of impacts from molecules of the water. In a follow-up paper to the initial relativity paper, also published in *Annalen der Physik* in 1905, Einstein announced a new result that he had deduced in the meantime, namely the interconvertibility of mass and energy through what became his signature equation, $E = mc^2$. All in all, then, this wasn't a bad year's output from the spare-time activity of a humble patent clerk!

During the course of the next couple of years, as the implications of Einstein's papers came increasingly to be recognised, and as he and others, most notably the mathematician Hermann Minkowski, gradually worked through some of the conceptual problems to which his work had given rise, his reputation rapidly expanded and so did his scientific situation.

In 1909, out of the blue, Einstein was awarded an honorary doctorate by the University of Geneva, in company with such scientific luminaries as Marie Curie and Wilhelm Ostwald. At more or less the same moment, he was appointed an associate professor at the University of Zürich. Two months later, in Salzburg, he gave his first invited lecture, on the quantum theory of radiation, to the cream of German physics at that year's congress of German scientists. In 1910, Einstein was nominated for the first time for the Nobel Prize in physics. In March 1911, he moved to a full chair at the German University in Prague; in August of the following year he returned to Zürich, this time to a chair in the Polytechnic Institute, the so-called ETH (Eidgenossische Technische Hochschule), a considerably more prestigious institution than either the university in Prague or the University of Zürich that he had left the previous year; and then in late 1913 he was appointed to a full-time research position in Berlin created especially for him, funded jointly by the newly-founded Kaiser-Wilhelm Institute for Physics and the Deutsche Akademie der Wissenschaften. In the space of a little over four years, he had risen from patent-office clerk to one of the most prestigious scientific appointments in all Germany!

While this was happening, Einstein had also been pursuing his research on the theory of relativity. The so-called special theory that he had announced in 1905 treated the way in which the laws of physics transformed between one frame of reference and another moving at constant speed relative to the first. Later, he sought to generalize the theory so as also to encompass the situation where the two frames of reference were accelerating with respect to each other. Such a situation was, he saw, from an analytical point of view equivalent to that of a body moving in a gravitational field, so that the theory he was pursuing promised to encompass the whole world as we know it. But the mathematics was very difficult – indeed, in cracking the problem, as he eventually did, Einstein had to learn a lot of new mathematics with which few physicists were familiar. (This was, no doubt, what lay behind the legend that I can remember hearing when I was growing up in the 1940s, ridiculous in fact but that had become part of the mystique surrounding Einstein, namely that the theory he had developed was so difficult that only a handful of people around the world could understand it.) A preliminary solution was announced in 1913, sufficient to prompt a German expedition to the Crimea in 1914, under the physicist Erwin Freundlich, to make observations during a solar eclipse that would be visible there, in the hope of confirming a prediction of the theory. Unfortunately, the expedition coincided with the outbreak of war; the expedition's equipment was impounded by the Russian authorities and Freundlich and his companions were arrested.

Not until 1916 was Einstein able to publish a fully satisfactory solution to the problem he had set himself. By then, of course, the war was set on its awful, murderous path. As soon as his paper was published in *Annalen der Physik*, effectively turning traditional Newtonian science on its head, he sent a copy to Wilhelm de Sitter, professor of astronomy at Leiden, in Holland, whom he had met on several occasions during the previous few years and with whom he had no problems in communicating since Holland was neutral during World War One. De Sitter was of course also able to communicate with people on the Allied side – in fact, he was the designated foreign correspondent of Britain's Royal Astronomical Society (RAS) – and he promptly sent Einstein's paper on to London, to the secretary of the RAS, A.S. Eddington, professor of astronomy at Cambridge. Eddington quickly mastered Einstein's paper and, realising its importance, commissioned De Sitter to prepare several articles for the RAS's journal, its *Monthly Notices of the Royal Astronomical Society*, explaining Einstein's theory. De Sitter wrote three long articles, his exposition benefiting from discussions with Einstein during a visit the latter paid to Leiden – and so, notwithstanding the difficulties in communication brought about by the war, the General Theory of Relativity, developed and first published in Berlin at the height of the war, quickly became known in Britain where Eddington became its chief proselytizer.[11]

Einstein was born in Ulm, in southern Germany, of German-Jewish parents, but at the age of 16, disgusted by the militaristic attitudes in the school he attended, he had renounced his German citizenship and gone to live in Switzerland. Officially stateless for several years, he eventually was able to take out Swiss citizenship, and he remained a Swiss citizen even after moving to Berlin. This had practical advantages for him during the war, making it easier for him to travel to neutral countries such as Switzerland, where his wife and children were living, or to Holland, than it might otherwise have been. But it also left him detached from the patriotic fervour that swept over many of his colleagues in Berlin following the outbreak of war – indeed, he remained an outspoken pacifist throughout the war years and afterwards. In October 1914, in response to Allied accusations of German atrocities following the invasion of neutral Belgium, many of Germany's leading intellectuals put their names to a declaration that became known as the 'Manifesto of the 93', denying that Germans had committed atrocities, professing Germany's innocence in causing the war, and asserting that Germany's culture and military tradition were one and the same. Einstein and a few others refused to sign the document and attempted to launch a counter-manifesto, but this fell flat. He was also a founding member of a small democratic reformist group, the Bund Neues Vaterland, that was banned by the German authorities in 1916. His views on the war were no doubt known to his Dutch friends and passed on by them to the British.

The Manifesto caused outrage among scientists on the Allied side, many of whom condemned the signatories as willing contributors to the evil culture that in their view had brought about and was now prosecuting the war; and this bitterness of feeling continued after the war and led to an on-going policy of ostracism of German science. When in 1919 the leading scientific academies of the Allied nations came together to form a new organization, the International Research Council, to promote international scientific co-operation, Germany and the other Central Powers were explicitly excluded; and well into the 1920s, German scientists were refused admittance to international meetings and organizations. In response, many German scientists imposed what amounted to a counter-blockade on Allied scientists. Eventually in 1926, the International Research Council repealed its exclusionary rule, but it was several more years before German scientific organizations were willing to join the Council.

Given the general hostility to all things German, the immediate enthusiasm displayed in England for Einstein's work is remarkable. Eddington was central to this, and he quickly aroused the interest of the Astronomer Royal, Sir Frank Dyson. The two men recognised that a solar eclipse that was to occur in 1919, would be visible from the South Atlantic, and would provide an ideal opportunity to make an empirical test of Einstein's theory – for only in events on an astronomical scale did the predictions made by Einstein's theory differ by an observable amount from those made by traditional Newtonian science. A central tenet of the new theory was that a light ray followed not a straight line but a 'world-line', the shortest path in a space now held to be curved, the curvature of which was affected by the presence of gravitating masses – in effect, a light ray would be bent as it passed a gravitating mass. If the mass were large enough – say, the Sun – and if the Earth were positioned such that light from a prominent star had to pass close by the Sun on its way to us, this light would be deflected by an amount that could be calculated. Normally, the light from the star would be completely drowned by the much greater amount of light emitted by the Sun, but during a total solar eclipse, the sunlight is blocked out by the intervening body of the Moon, and so the star might be seen just off the limb of the obscured Sun, and its apparent position measured, and this position compared to the position determined when the Sun was not in the vicinity of the line of sight to the star. If the star-light was being deflected by the Sun, as Einstein's theory said it should be, the position measured during the eclipse should be different, and by a definite amount.

Despite the logistical difficulties arising from the war, Dyson and Eddington set to, to organize twin expeditions, one to the island of Principe, in the Gulf of Guinea and to be led by Eddington himself, the other to Sobral, on the other side of the Atlantic in Brazil. In March 1917, the British Government allocated the necessary funds. In January 1919, photographs were taken of the stars selected for the crucial observations against a reference frame of other stars. And on 29 May, when the eclipse occurred, excellent photographs were taken at both sites. The photographic plates were then measured, the observed positions of the selected stars being compared to their positions on the reference photographs taken earlier. Painstaking calculations were required to ensure that the results were dependable. Rumours were soon circulating but it was some time before Dyson and Eddington were sure of their ground and prepared to officially announce, at a joint meeting of the Royal Society and the Royal Astronomical Society held on 6 November 1919, that their results showed deflection of the light, and by just the amount that Einstein's theory had predicted. The famous physicist J.J. Thomson, the discoverer of the electron, was in the chair as President of the Royal Society. Einstein's theory, he declared in introducing Dyson to present the results, was 'one of the greatest achievements in the history of human thought ... Not the discovery of an outlying island but of a whole continent of new scientific ideas. It is the greatest discovery in connection with gravitation since Newton enunciated his principles'. As *The Times* put it in a leading article the next morning, 'the scientific conception of the fabric of the Universe must be changed'.

The report in *The Times* was just the start of what can only be described as a wave of hysteria in the press. In Berlin, journalists laid siege to Einstein's home; everywhere, reporters sought out people who could comment knowledgeably on what Einstein had achieved and explain it in terms that were comprehensible to ordinary people. Einstein, suddenly, was the most famous scientist in the world. The esoteric character of his theory was surely part of its attraction, and its alleged overturning of common sense, of everything people had thought they understood about the universe. But there was another factor at work, as well. Eddington was obviously excited by the beauty and power of Einstein's theory; but he was also a Quaker, deeply opposed to the war and eager to heal the divisions it had opened up between scientists on the two sides of the conflict. Dyson was the son of a Baptist pastor and deeply committed to his faith. Einstein as we have seen was also a pacifist, a 'good German' known not to share the sabre-rattling sympathies of the signatories to the 'Manifesto of the 93'; hence he and his work did not share in the opprobrium directed to the rest of German science at the time. (The fact that, technically speaking, he was not a German at all, was not widely recognised.) So far as Eddington was concerned then, and probably Dyson as well, to provide empirical confirmation for Einstein's theory was both of the first importance from a purely scientific point of view, and an ideal basis on which to affirm the traditional internationalist values of the Republic of Letters. As a result of their work, for Einstein at least, the strategy succeeded; all doors were opened, he was lionized wherever he went and maybe hearts were softened elsewhere to some extent, and among the general public. If they were, however, it was to a much smaller extent than Eddington might have hoped for. To illustrate: in 1920, when the first Solvay Conference – the exclusive gatherings of the world's top physicists – to be held after the war was being organized, Einstein was the only physicist from Germany who was invited. As the secretary put it while explaining that Germans were not being invited: 'an exception has been made for Einstein, of ill-defined nationality, Swiss I believe, who was roundly abused in Berlin during the war because of his pacifist sentiments which have never varied for a moment'. Einstein planned to attend, but in the end didn't do so because he went on a lecturing tour in America instead, to raise money for the Zionist cause in which he had become a strong believer. He was invited to attend the next conference as well, in 1923, but this time he declined the invitation because, he said, it would not be right for him to attend while his colleagues continued to be excluded. And, as pointed out already, even in such a supposedly apolitical business as science, it took a lot longer before the hostilities engendered by the war abated to the point where the traditional open dialogue could resume.

What we are left with is surely, however, a nice picture in itself, of a pacifist Quaker astronomer undertaking a major scientific expedition in the immediate aftermath of a catastrophic war, in pursuit of an arcane idea developed by another pacifist in the middle of war-torn Berlin at the height of the hostilities. And, succeeding in his quest and in the process transforming our understanding of the foundations of the world in which we live!

Epilogue

Not everyone was convinced by the data presented by Dyson and Eddington and, even among those who were, there was widespread agreement that further confirmation of their conclusions was required from observations during future solar eclipses. Here Australia played a role, because the next full eclipse would be in 1922 and would be visible in a band stretching across Australia from Wallal on the northwest coast to Goondiwindi in southern Queensland. To observe it, the Adelaide Observatory organized an expedition to Cordillo Downs, in the far north-east of South Australia. The Sydney Observatory arranged an expedition to Goondiwindi, and the Lick Observatory in California organized an expedition to Wallal. All sought to test Einstein's prediction. The Lick Observatory team was the best equipped to make the observations required; the results obtained fully confirmed those obtained by Eddington three years earlier.[12]

Notes

1 The 12th International Congress of Biochemistry, held in Perth in August 1982.

2 G.D. Beer, *The Sciences Were Never at War* (London: Nelson, 1960).

3 Jacques-Julien Houtou de La Billardière, *Novae Hollandiae plantarum specimen ...* (Paris: Lehre, 1804).

4 D. Stoltzenberg, *Fritz Haber, Chemist, Nobel Laureate, German, Jew: a Biography* (Philadelphia: Chemical Heritage Press, 2004).

5 R. MacLeod, 'The "Arsenal" in The Strand: Australian Chemists and the British Munitions Effort, 1916–1919', *Annals of Science*, 46 (1989), 45–67.

6 W. Hackmann, *Seek and Strike: Anti-Submarine Warfare and the Royal Navy, 1914–54* (London: HMSO, 1984).

7 J. Jenkin, *William and Lawrence Bragg, Father and Son: the Most Extraordinary Collaboration in Science* (Oxford: Oxford University Press, 2008), 368–86.

8 There is a vast number of studies of Einstein and his work. For the most part I have drawn on R. Clark, *Einstein, the Life and Times* (New York: A.A. Knopf, 1971); A. Pais, *'Subtle Is the Lord...': the Science and the Life of Albert Einstein* (Oxford: Clarendon Press, 1982), and F. Stern, *Einstein's German World* (Princeton: Princeton University Press, 1999), esp. ch. 3. The best recent biography is A. Fölsing, *Albert Einstein: a Biography* (New York & London: Viking, 1997).

9 R.W. Home, 'William Sutherland and the 'Sutherland-Einstein' Diffusion Relation: Theoretical Physics in a Colonial Setting', *Historia Scientiarum*, 15 (2005), 125–38.

10 On the award of the Nobel Prize to Einstein, see Pais, ch. 30.

11 Eddington's role in promoting the theory is described in Matthew Stanley's *Practical Mystic: Religion, Science and A.S. Eddington* (Chicago: University of Chicago Press, 2007), ch. 3, and more extensively in Stanley's *Einstein's War: How Relativity Conquered Nationalism and Shook the World* (New York/London, 2019), copies of which first reached Australia after the present paper was written.

12 J. Crelinsten, 'William Wallace Campbell and the 'Einstein Problem': an Observational Astronomer Confronts the Theory of Relativity', *Historical Studies in the Physical Sciences*, 14 (1983), 1–91.

1919
A Chronology

The work of physicist Ernest Rutherford on the splitting of nitrogen atoms appeared in four papers in the *Philosophical Magazine* in the first half of 1919, the key one in June.

January: Spartacist uprising in Berlin is suppressed and leaders Karl Liebknecht and Rosa Luxemburg are murdered.

In January 1919 the Australian Farmers' Federal Organization (forerunner of the Country Party 1925) adopts principles derived from State farmers' and settlers' unions or associations.

13 January: Peace Conference opens in Versailles with W.M. Hughes and Sir Joseph Cook as Australia's delegates.

14 January: Germany releases Allied POWs.

mid-January: The global influenza pandemic first enters the Australian community, in Melbourne.

16 January: ratification of the 18th Amendment to US Constitution (prohibition came into force a year later).

21 January: Dáil Éireann, comprising 25 Sinn Féin members elected in the 1918 general election but who, in accordance with their declaration of an Irish Republic have not taken their seats in the UK Parliament, meets for the first time in the Mansion House, Dublin. In the first shots of the Anglo-Irish war, two Royal Irish Constabulary men are ambushed and killed at Soloheadbeg in County Tipperary.

23 January: 150,000 UK miners joined nationwide strikes for a shorter working week; miners reject government terms on 12 February.

27 January: general ironworkers strike in Glasgow and Belfast.

27 January: following the arrival of the troop ship Sardinia in Sydney, eight of whose passengers had died from influenza, NSW is proclaimed a quarantine area.

31 January: riots and protests against high rents in George Square, Glasgow, are met by the army with tanks.

February: civil war in Russia and Allied invasion.

3 February: Sinn Féin leader Éamon de Valera and two other prisoners escape from Lincoln Prison.

4 February: Melbourne's Royal Exhibition Building becomes an influenza hospital.

5 February: United Artists film studio established by Charles Chaplin, Douglas Fairbanks, D.W. Griffith and Mary Pickford.

6–11 February: General strike of 65,000 in Seattle, where strikers take over the city government. Ends after one week as thousands of federal troops and special deputies are mobilised by authorities.

14 February: Wilson's proposal for a League of Nations is accepted.

19 February: W.E.B. Du Bois-organised Pan African Congress meets in Paris.

19 February: attempted assassination of President Clemenceau.

20 February: communist revolt breaks out in Budapest.

22 February: a Soviet Republic is proclaimed in Bavaria, the day after the murder of Premier Eisner.

27 February: first public performance of Gustav Holst's The Planets.

March: Japan suppresses peaceful demonstrations for Korean independence; Egyptian uprisings against British rule.

1 March: *Smith's Weekly* commences publication in Sydney.

2–6 March 1919: the Communist International (Comintern) (First Congress/Third International) met in Moscow.

3 March: German Communists proclaim a general strike (crushed by March 11).

10 March: Commonwealth Government offers £10,000 prize to the first Australian crew to fly a British-made aircraft from Britain to Australia in 30 days, before the end of 1919.

23 March: Benito Mussolini forms *Fasci di Combattimento* ('combat groups') in Milan.

23 March: Bolsheviks march in Brisbane demanding civil liberties and the repeal of the War Precautions Act.

24 March: returned soldiers lead several thousand 'anti-Bolsheviks' against Bolsheviks and the Russian Association offices in Brisbane.

30 March: Mahatma Gandhi initiates non-violence campaigns.

April:

5 April: Eamon de Valera is elected president of Sin Fein.

7 April: 'Original Dixieland Jazz Band' arrives in London for a 15-month tour.

10 April: Emiliano Zapata, a leader of the Mexican peasant revolt against dictatorship, is killed.

11 April: attempt to overthrow the Bavarian Soviet.

13 April: Amritsar Massacre in the Punjab Province, British India: British and Ghurkha troops kill 379 Sikhs and injure more than 1,200.

19 April: UK government announces more troops for Egypt to counter nationalist unrest.

May:

1 May: May Day clash in Cleveland between protesters at the gaoling of Eugene V. Debs and Victory Liberty Loan Workers.

3 May: Hungarian communist regime surrenders.

3 May: Victorian Football Association resumes its 10-team fixture, the first full-length season since 1914, and the League opens its season with nine teams.

4 May: May 4th Movement in China proclaims a 'struggle for sovereignty' to 'throw out the warlord traitors'.

4–8 May: striking wharf labourers, non-unionist strike-breakers and police engage in the 'Battle of the Barricades' on Fremantle's waterfront.

5 May 1919: beginning of the Greco-Turkish War of 1919–1922.

14 May: the AIF cricket team begins its successful tour of England that brings to prominence a number of future Australian Test players.

15 May: the body of Nurse Edith Cavell, returned from Belgium, is re-interred at Norwich.

19 May 1919–November 1920: strike closes the Broken Hill mines closed by strike.

19 May–26 August: seamen's strike halts most shipping around Australia.

28 May: Australia's first electric train service operates (Essendon–Sandringham).

29 May: observations at Príncipe and at Sobral, Brazil, during a full solar eclipse, test Einstein's general theory of relativity (confirmed by the Royal Astronomical Society on 19 November).

June: In Brussels, Joseph Cardijn, Fernand Tonnet and others formed groups of *La Jeunesse Syndicaliste,* Young Trade Unionists, which in 1924 became *Jeunesse Ouvrière Chrétienne*, the Young Christian Workers.

4 June: US Congress passes the 19th Amendment making it illegal to deny women the right to vote.

21 June: on the orders of Admiral Ludwig von Reuter, the interned German fleet is scuttled in Scapa Flow, Scotland.

28 June: W.M. Hughes and Sir Joseph Cook sign the Treaty of Versailles for Australia, incorporating a draft Covenant of League of Nations.

29 June: nine striking Brisbane meatworkers are wounded in a clash with police.

July:

4 July: Jack Dempsey wins the world heavyweight championship.

12 July: the Allies lift their blockade on Germany.

18 July 1919: unveiling of Edwin Lutyens' (temporary, wood-and-plaster) Cenotaph in Whitehall, preceding the London Victory / Peace Parade on 19 July.

19 July: Peace Day parades throughout the British Empire; in England, rioting UK ex-servicemen burn down Luton Town Hall.

19 July: Melbourne's Peace Day procession is followed by clashes between returned soldiers and police.

21 July: returned servicemen, demonstrating against police heavy-handedness, assault Victorian Premier Harry Lawson during their invasion of government offices.

31 July: the Weimar Republic is declared.

31 July: a police strike in London and Liverpool for union recognition leads to riots in Liverpool and the dismissal of over 2,000 strikers.

31 July: UK Housing, Town Planning &c. Act 1919 provides government subsidies for the provision of council houses, the target being 500,000 houses by 1922.

27 July–3 August: Chicago race riots.

August:

19 August: Afghanistan gains independence from the UK (after the Third Afghan War, May–August 1919).

20 August: the wartime measure of six o'clock closing of Melbourne hotels becomes permanent.

24 August: Prime Minister W.M. Hughes arrives back in Australia.

30 August: the UK Football League is resumed after four years' suspension.

31 August: General Jan Smuts succeeds Louis Botha as South African PM.

September: Moving approval of the Versailles Treaties in the Australian Parliament, PM Hughes claims credit for Australia's separate representation at Versailles, for obtaining the New Guinea Mandate on 'C Class' terms, and for the defeat of the Japanese 'racial equality' clause, but admits that he had not obtained the reparations that he thought due.

10 September: death of J.F. Archibald, who leaves part of his estate for an annual prize for portraiture.

12 September: leader Adolf Hitler addresses a meeting of the German Workers' Party in Munich.

19 September: official launching of Victoria's Great Ocean Road project, using the labour of returned soldiers.

20 September: aided by the introduction of preferential voting in 1918, the second Farmers' Union-endorsed candidate wins a seat in the House of Representatives.

22 September: President Wilson, campaigning in the Mid West for support of the Peace Treaty, suffers a complete breakdown.

22 September: a nationwide steel strike begins in the United States, with 365,000 workers walking out. The strike was defeated after three and a half months on 8 January 1920.

27 September: the last British troops leave Archangel, Russia.

27 September: Footscray 8.17 (65) defeated minor premiers North Melbourne 6.7 (43) in the VFA Grand Final at East Melbourne Cricket Ground before a crowd of 20,000.

October:

4 October: premiere at Melbourne Town Hall of Raymond Longford's film *The Sentimental Bloke.*

7 October: death of Alfred Deakin; birth of Zelman Cowen.

11 October: Collingwood 11.12 (78) defeated Richmond 7.11 (53) in the VFL Grand Final at the Melbourne Cricket Ground before a crowd of 45,413.

14 October: in London, Australian Oscar Asche's musical extravaganza *Chu Chin Chow* sets a world record of 1,467 performances.

20 October: VC winner Albert Jacka receives an enthusiastic welcome home in Melbourne.

21 October: report of the imminent victory of the Red Army over the White Russians.

27 October: premiere in London of Edward Elgar's Cello Concerto.

November: D.H. Lawrence exiled himself from England; *Women in Love* was published in 1920.

2 November: 500,000 US coal workers strike for substantial pay rises and shorter working hours.

4 November: Artilleryman wins the Melbourne Cup.

11 November: Armistice Day is inaugurated with a two-minute silence.

12 November: Ross and Keith Smith commence their flight to Australia in a Vickers-Vimy aircraft.

19 November: the US Senate rejects the Treaty of Versailles.

(In October 1920 President Wilson was awarded the 1919 Nobel Prize for Peace.)

19 November: British government grants Egypt a constitution.

19 November: following the socialist election victory, Benito Mussolini and 37 fascists are arrested.

26 November: the State Electricity Commission of Victoria decides to establish a powerhouse on the Morwell brown coalfield in the Latrobe Valley.

28 November: official inauguration of the building of the Mitta Mitta Dam (renamed the Hume Weir in 1920, and the Hume Dam in 1996).

30 November: women vote for the first time in French general elections.

December:

1 December: Nancy Astor, Viscountess Astor, elected on 8 November, takes her seat in the House of Commons, succeeding her husband as the Unionist member for Plymouth Sutton.

10 December: the US coal miners strike ends.

10 December: carrying the first overseas airmail between England and Australia, Ross and Keith Smith land at Darwin and win the air race.

13 December: the House of Representatives and half Senate election is contested by three parties (Nationalists, Labor and a farmers' party) and won by the Nationalists; two referenda to extend the Commonwealth's wartime powers are rejected.

19 December: General Sir William Birdwood and Major General Sir John Monash arrive in Perth, and in Melbourne on 26 December.

19 December: attempted assassination of the Lord Lieutenant of Ireland outside Phoenix Park, Dublin.

21 December: anarchist Emma Goldman is deported from US to Russia.

22 December: a Bill 'to provide for the better government of Ireland' is introduced in the House of Commons, providing for parliaments in Dublin and Belfast, in accordance with the Cabinet's Irish Committee policy (2 November) of separate Home Rule parliaments for Ulster's six counties and the other 26 counties.

23 December: the U.K. Sex Disqualification (Removal) Act abolishes legal disabilities on women entering the secular professions. One week later Lincoln's Inn, London, admits its first female bar student.

Contributors

Dr Anthea Hyslop taught history at the Australian National University from 1989 to 2009, and before that at the universities of Adelaide and Melbourne, and at La Trobe University where she gained her PhD. She specialises in the social history of medicine, and is writing a book on Australia's experience of the Spanish influenza pandemic of 1918–1919.

Emeritus Professor Roderick W. Home was Professor of History and Philosophy of Science at the University of Melbourne, 1975–2003, and has been Emeritus Professor since 2003. Rod has written extensively on the history of physics, especially in the eighteenth century, and on the history of science in Australia.

Associate Professor John Lack is a Principal Fellow in the School of Historical and Philosophical Studies at the University of Melbourne, where he taught Australian history for 25 years. He has written and edited several books, including *A History of Footscray* and his late colleague Jacqueline Templeton's outstanding *From the Mountains to the Bush.* Most recently John has published articles in the *Victorian Historical Journal* and *The La Trobe Journal* about family and community life on the fraught Australian home front during the Great War,

Dr Ross McMullin is an independent historian and biographer. His book *Pompey Elliott* was awarded prizes for biography and literature, and his other books include *Will Dyson: Australia's Radical Genius*, and the commissioned centenary history of the ALP, *The Light on the Hill.* His multi-biography *Farewell, Dear People: Biographies of Australia's Lost Generation* was awarded the Prime Minister's Prize for Australian History. His most recent book is *Pompey Elliott at War: In His Own Words*. http://www.rossmcmullin.com.au

Dr David Palmer is a Visiting Associate at SHAPS at the University of Melbourne. He is the author of *Organizing the Shipyards: Union Strategy in Three Northeast Ports, 1933–1945*, the chapter 'Foreign Forced Labor at Mitsubishi's Nagasaki and Hiroshima Shipyards' in Marcel van der Linden and Magaly Rodriguez Garcia (eds), *On Coerced Labour: Work and Compulsion after Chattel Slavery*, and other publications on the history of labour in the U.S., Japan, and Australia.

Dr Val Noone was during the 1960s a chaplain to YCW groups in several Melbourne suburbs. These days he is a Fellow in the School of Historical and Philosophical Studies at the University of Melbourne, and has published on the Irish in Victoria and also post-1945 Australian Catholicism.

Dr Carolyn Rasmussen has worked as a public historian since 1985, ranging over the history of Victorian public institutions, the labour movement, science and technology, education, and biography. She is currently an Honorary Fellow in the University of Melbourne and chair of the Victorian Working Party of the *Australian Dictionary of Biography*. Her most recent publication is *The Blackburns: Private Lives, Public Ambition.*

Dr Tony Ward has been a Fellow in the School of Historical and Philosophical Studies at the University of Melbourne since 2011. He has published widely in Australian history, sports history, and social economics. His two books are *Sport in Australian National Identity* and *Bridging Troubled Waters: Australia and Asylum Seekers*, and he has published in journals including *Australian Economic Review* and *Sporting Traditions.*

Dr Fay Woodhouse is a professional historian who has written histories of Australian businesses, universities, and community organisations, and biographies of Melbourne personalities. She is a contributor to the *Australian Dictionary of Biography.* Her research interests include early Melbourne, the 1930s, and the 1950s, and she is currently completing a history of Melbourne's first yoga school. Fay is an Honorary Fellow in the School of Historical and Philosophical Studies at the University of Melbourne.

The SHAPS Fellows & Associates Group was formed in 2005 when a group of retired academics, historians, classicists and archaeologists began monthly meetings to discuss their current research. All continue to publish books, chapters of books, journal articles, book reviews and entries in Australian and international dictionaries of biography as well as in various online journals and other forums. In their second year of association, the SHAPS Fellows & Associates instigated an annual Research Day for the presentation of work-in-progress papers about their recent or forthcoming publications. The monthly seminars and the Fellows & Associates Research Day, popular forums for intellectual and social interactions within the School, encourage the participation of postgraduates and members of the historical profession. Dr Prue Torney, one of the founding members of the Fellows Group, who was tragically killed in 2006, has been remembered since 2011 by the combined Fellows & Associates – SHAPS Prue Torney Memorial Prize. In 2013 the Fellows & Associates Group established an annual history essay prize for journal articles published by SHAPS postgraduates.

Printed in Australia
Ingram Content Group Australia Pty Ltd
AUHW020840101024
401057AU00002B/47

9 781925 984156